Lying Like Presidents

Critical praise for
Djelloul Marbrook's fiction

Suffer the Children:
Ludilon (a short novel) & Sailing Her Navel (poems)
(2019, Leaky Boot Press)

… gives the reader—through virtuosic poetry and prose—a devastating portrait of child abuse and its life-long consequences. This brave, stunning, and incisive dissection of the damage that permeates the entire lives of the abused and the abuser rings with raw power. The child and adult voices of Pip and Sally will echo indelibly in the reader's mind. A masterpiece.

—Roselee Blooston, author of *Dying in Dubai: A Memoir of Marriage, Mourning and the Middle East* (2016) & *Trial by Family* (2019)

Guest Boy, Book 1, Light Piercing Water trilogy
(2018, Leaky Boot Press)

What Marbrook does so well in *Guest Boy* is the contradictory elegance he showed in *Saraceno*. He finds the tender and poetic heart of very tough men. In *Saraceno*, it was low-level mobsters; in *Guest Boy*, it's men of the sea. They're a horny-handed bunch, and Marbrook's familiarity with ships and the characters of mean-street ports is deep and exciting. But Marbrook knows that these guys have a lot more going on within, and are simultaneously deeply tender philosophers. It's a mesmerizing book… You'll find yourself thinking about it long after you've finished reading.

—Dan Baum, author of *Gun Guys* (2013), *Nine Lives* (2009), and others

Guest Boy is a complex work: deep, passionate, exciting and beautifully written with flashbacks and imagery merging real and surreal. By opening up routes to the culture and history of the Arab world, *Guest Boy* helps us understand that world and our own.

—Sanford Fraser, author of *Tourist* and *Among Strangers I've Known All My Life*

Artemisia's Wolf
(title story, *A Warding Circle,* 2017, Leaky Boot Press)

… Djelloul Marbrook's impressive novella … successfully blends humor and satire (and perhaps even a touch of magic realism) into its short length … an engrossing story, but what might strike the reader most throughout the book is its infusion of breathtaking poetry … a stunning rebuke to notoriously misogynist subcultures like the New York art scene…

—Tommy Zurhellen (author of the award-winning *Messiah Trilogy*), *Hudson River Valley Review*

… lets his powerful imagination run wild, leading the fiction into unexpected corners where weird performers hold court and produce endings that both astonish and are frequently magical.

—James Polk, *The Country and Abroad,* former contributing editor of *Art/World*.

Saraceno
(2012, Bliss Plot Press)

Djelloul Marbrook writes dialogue that not only entertains with an intoxicating clickety-clack, but also packs a truth about low-life mob culture "The Sopranos" only hints at. You can practically smell the anisette and filling-station coffee.

—Dan Baum, author of *Gun Guys* (2013), *Nine Lives* (2009), and others

... a good ear for crackling dialogue ... I love Marbrook's crude, raw music of the streets. The notes are authentic and on target ...

—Sam Coale, *The Providence (RI) Journal*

... an entirely new variety of gangster tale ... a Mafia story sculpted with the most refined of sensibilities from the clay of high art and philosophy . .. the kind of writer I take real pleasure in discovering ... a mature artist whose rich body of work is finally coming to light.

—Brent Robison, editor, *Prima Materia*

Alice Miller's Room
(title story, *Making Room*, 2017, Leaky Boot Press)

This enchanting novella is a delicately wrought homage to Jung's famous principle of meaningful coincidence...

—Phil Boxall, *Breakfast All Day,* UK

... the story draws us into that mysterious and terrifying realm where the heart will have its say and all who enter leave transformed...

—Dr. Patricia L. Divine, Head Start program lifetime service award winner

Mean Bastards Making Nice (2014, Leaky Boot Press)

I love it. I admire it. It is you at your best.

—Best-selling novelist Gail Godwin, on "The Pain of Wearing Our Faces"

☙

Critical praise for
Djelloul Marbrook's poetry

Far from Algiers (2008, Kent State University Press)

... as succinct as most stanzas by Dickinson... an unusually mature, confidently composed first poetry collection.

—Susanna Roxman, *Prairie Schooner*
(author of *Crossing the North Sea*)

... brings together the energy of a young poet with the wisdom of long experience.

—Edward Hirsch, Guggenheim Foundation

... honors a lifetime of hidden achievement.

—Toi Derricotte, Wick Award judge

. . . wise and flinty poems outfox the furies of exile, prejudice, and longing... a remarkable and distinctive debut.

—Cyrus Cassells, National Poetry Series winner

Brash Ice (2014, Leaky Boot Press)

. . . resonates with wisdom and a keen eye for the beautiful things of this world . . .a poetry that would make brash ice melt again.

—George Drew, author of *The View From Jackass Hill*

… a precision that occasionally recalls Yeats …

—James Polk, *The Country and Abroad*

Brushstrokes and glances (2010, Deerbrook Editions)

Whether it is commentary on state power, corporate greed, or the intensely personal death of a loved one, Djelloul Marbrook is clear sighted, eloquent, and precise. As the title of the collection suggests, he uses the lightest touch, a collection of fragments, brushstrokes and glances, to fashion poems that resonate with truth and honesty.

—Phil Constable, *New York Journal of Books*

... looks at art the way a drinker drinks—deeply, passionately, and desperately, as if his life depended on it … makes you want to run out to your favorite museum and look again, as you have never looked before, until the lights go out.

—Barbara Louise Ungar, author of *Thrift*; *Charlotte Brontë, You Ruined My Life*; *The Origin of the Milky Way*

… one of those colossal poets able to bridge worlds—poetry and art, heart and mind—with rare wit, grace, and sincerity; a soft-spoken artist with the courage to face the "fatal beckoning" of his muse … crisp intellect, seamlessly interwoven with loss and longing. … poetry at its best: at once both gritty and refined, private and political, tender and tough as iron … well worth reading."

—Michael Meyerhofer, author of *What to do if you're buried alive*, *Damnatio Memoriae*, *Blue Collar Eulogies*

…delicately wrought… highly recommended reading…because, ultimately, this witness so clearly loves his subject.

—Eileen Tabios, Editor, *Galatea Resurrects*

Riding Thermals to Winter Grounds (2017, Leaky Boot Press)

… some very powerful lines, such as: "And then, near the end of my life, I become the man I wanted to be without the fuss and bother of giving a damn."

—Sidney Grayling, editor, Onager Editions

I don't know anyone else whose writing increases in agility and breadth over time as Marbrook's does.

—Lee Gould, editor, *La Presa*, the Embajadoro Press poetry journal

Lying Like Presidents

New and selected poems
2001-2019

Djelloul Marbrook

LEAKY BOOT PRESS

Lying like presidents
New and selected poems 2001-2019
by Djelloul Marbrook

Acknowledgments

Three excerpts from "Lying Like Presidents" appeared in *La Presa*, the
Embajadoro Press journal (Mexico): "If he hadn't stared (poem 12)" and "I
hope for an unimaginable species (poem 18)" in No. 7, Spring 2019, and
"Disgrace (poem 14)" in No. 8, Fall 2019.
"What good did my own good do me?" in *Far from Algiers* appeared
in *American Poetry Review*, November-December 2008.
"That first kiss" in *Air Tea with Dolores* appeared in *Le Zaporogue* No. 9
(Denmark), December 2010.
"I worked in a taxidermy studio" in *Air Tea with Dolores* appeared in
The Ledge Poetry and Fiction Magazine, Winter 2009-10, and in
The Country and Abroad, June 2008.

ISBN: 978-1-909849-82-2 (softcover)
ISBN: 978-1-909849-86-0 (hardcover)

First published in 2020 by Leaky Boot Press
Copyright © 2020 Djelloul Marbrook

A full CIP record for this book is available from the British
Library in the UK and from the Library of Congress in the USA.

"We are all born ignorant,
but one must work hard
to remain stupid."

—Benjamin Franklin

For Efrem M. Ostrowsky, dear friend

(May 29, 1919–April 21, 2009)

Author's Acknowledgments

Endless thanks are owed to my wife, Marilyn, who has in so many ways made all my work possible; to James Goddard, my publisher, whose steadfast faith in my work brought it to light and buoyed me in rough waters; to Sebastien Doubinsky, who published my work and introduced me to James Goddard; to Toi Derricotte, whose selection of *Far From Algiers* for the Stan and Tom Wick Poetry Award gave me confidence to continue; to Brent Robison, whose wizardly videos and deft hand with e-books still astonish me; to Kevin Swanwick, whose radiance as a reader and advisor unfailingly enlightens me, and to Emily Brooks, whose artistic taste, good cheer and resourcefulness seem fathomless.

Contents

selections from *Riding Thermals to Winter Grounds*

selections from *Air Tea with Dolores*

selections from *Nothing True Has a Name*

selections from *Even Now the Embers*

selections from *Other Risks Include*

selections from *The Seas Are Dolphins' Tears*

selections from *Singing in the O of Not*

selections from *The Loneliness of Shape*

selections from *Suffer the Children: Sailing Her Navel*

At a certain age the gloomy among us may wonder if this is their last suit, their last pair of shoes. Lifting such gloom has been my Sisyphean task, and so the idea of a book of selected poems strikes me as essentially funereal. Are these the duds, the shoes, the book I should be buried with?

In some ways I have been both family undertaker and archaeologist, and what I have uncovered reminds me of the Elgin marbles; they should be returned to the Hellenes. Without explanation. They explain themselves. So should my poems. And that's where the gloom lifts, in my recognition that their underlying impulse is to divorce Wikipedia, birth certificate, DNA, awards, black marks, the apparatus and paraphernalia by which we define ourselves.

They should have been anonymous; I should have had the courage to let them be. Would they then have been published at all? I should have grappled with such questions earlier, and yet I know that one way or another I've grappled with them from the beginning. *Far From Algiers*, my first collection of poems, addresses alienation, rootlessness and anonymity. But it's a kind of jeremiad, while ten books later the issue becomes an observance if not celebration with the publication of *The Loneliness of Shape* and *Singing in the O of Not*, which might be described as poems of disappearance.

It would be easy if not pretentious to claim this interest in anonymity is rooted in Sufic studies and the idea that the job of the dervish is to disappear. The whirling dervishes, for example, whirl away their egos. But for me it's rooted in a privet chapel in a boarding school in West Islip, New York, where I prayed skyward for deliverance from rape, molestation and abuse. It is in that chapel where I left the child called Djelloul and went on as someone else, only to hear him late in my life calling for reunion. In some ways these poems are an act of communion with that dismayed boy. If they emit any light at all it derives from that alchemy. Communion and alchemy—they're as synonymous as they're disparate in my mind, the one aspiring, the other ennobling.

The title poem, "Lying Like Presidents," is in some ways an orgiastic celebration of the recovery of that child. The recovery itself is described in *Suffer the Children,* consisting of a novella called "Ludilon" and a collection of poems called "Sailing her navel." Here Sally and Pip recount their sexual ordeal at the hands of Aisling Wynant, a young war widow. They discover that they can't tell each other as adults what they have made of that ordeal without giving Aisling a voice, even if they must only imagine what she might say.

I did not think I would survive the writing of *Suffer the Children.* At times I did not think I should survive it. Now I am not sure I did survive it. But I knew I had to listen to Sally, Pip and Aisling, and that meant at times playing the role of an ancient Egyptian priest calling forth voices from statues. I had to bear to hear exactly what I had lived most of my life not wanting to hear. It meant rediscovering Sally, whom I had erased from memory, a girl who shapes my responses to all women as much as Aisling does. There were times when I could hardly bear to hear Sally. There were times when Aisling horrified me even more than she had when I was helpless in her hands.

When I was done, perhaps after a week or two, the linked cantos that comprise "Lying Like Presidents" began to clamor for each other. At first they seemed to me disparate, unrelated. But after I had written some thirty or more manuscript pages their linkages began blinking like signals. I soon recognized their echolalia; they were repeating key refrains of previous poems. The primary meaning of echolalia posits that the repetition be meaningless; these poems were not, because they summoned succeeding poems. But the secondary meaning of echolalia is repetition for the sake of learning, and I was learning. I was listening far more than I was writing. I was listening, learning, hurting and celebrating, celebrating having reunited with Sally and Aisling to comprehend what we had meant to each other, what we meant now. The poems kept coming, even when I thought the project finished. Each key phrase and idea echoed in following poems until the poems were talking to each other. Towards the end I remembered that there were two beloved friends in my childhood who repeated the last words or phrases of whatever they spoke. I remembered that I had loved this trait, that it had influenced my entire output as a poet, that it had seemed magical, eerie, sacred even. I had loved Peter and Dolores for their speech as much as I had loved them for their looks and our companionship. They haunt *Lying like presidents;* they are its honored guests.

A poem is, whatever else it is, a recollection, and I am keenly attuned to this notion because since my adolescence I have been beset by periodic bouts of amnesia, an aspect of trauma. I never know what my mind will throw out. It could be the skill to drive. Once in my late thirties it was my job skills. Some memories return; others are lost. My poems are always in some sense a search for the lost, but when what has been lost is found it is never quite its former self, and so reacquaintance is an element of these poems. What do I now make of what I once remembered well? I think of this as a welcoming of ghosts, but they have their own minds and wonts, and I am as much their guest as they are mine.

I step aside for them. I leave my luggage at the airport in the hope it will be lost. I step out of my disguises. I leave my doodads, gimcracks and gewgaws in the locker of a station or an airport I have only dreamed. That is my conceit, anyway. In this sense, these poems written from 2001 to 2019 chart a trek from a betrayed boy who becomes a scared drunk, a flawed husband and father, mad idealist, golem, to a fairly decent old man who sometimes passes like fume through keyholes and under doors, or imagines he does. Sometimes he scrawls what he at least is pleased to call a poem with a child's forefinger on a frosty windowpane.

—*Djelloul Marbrook, January 2019*

Lying Like Presidents

Yesterday eighty years ago I toddled on the brink
of catastrophe, and the world tottered with me
in Flushing Meadows, toddled, tottered, teetered,
then fell between the trylon and perisphere,
orange and blue happiness in Peggy's arms,
on Dorothy's shoulders, in Grandma's smile,
fell to bits that repelled each other.
Millions were already dying, I was only
miles away from rape and body parts
I have never been able to reassemble, miles away
from that great gurgling sump in West Islip
where I was disassembled by dissemblers
eighty years ago east of Babylon, west
of that great mistake from which I came
blue-veiled, nameless, Semtex ticking
like Earth on its shook axis, already dying,
stars screeching, oceans writhing, there
in Flushing Meadows, no getting back
to Brooklyn, no safety left for any of us
after the hot dogs and ice cream,
the faces that didn't have to be read
to mete the proper measure of dread.
Nothing ever impended then,
nothing ever would feel safe again.

We got a little tired towards the end

We all have lost that moment
when something might have happened
that would have led anywhere but here,
lost, thrown away, ritually interred,
but mostly I've been busy addressing
rumors of my existence, bigfooting
like Sasquatch or a yeti through
squalls of others' suppositions,
maelstroms, melees of my own,
brushing away cobwebs of attempts
to swing on this or that strand
toward a moment I did inhabit
only to find husks of might have been,
lost that moment when breathlessly
I might get the right word out.
What would the right word have been
and didn't I occasionally say it,
turning someone inside out, proving
I'm always about to say that one thing
you depend on not hearing?
What would it have been been,
and does it even matter now
that I can't remember it? Here's the face,
right here in this crossfire of eyebeams,
that hasn't seen light for thousands of years
and now stares down the sun
while you drop your shovels and picks
on your toes and turn to lecture students
about all you don't understand.
Not just this face, but the child's
you molested, the wife you raped,
the voters you fooled, all of them
that for some reason you can't see,
that reason being what you live to dispel

If I speak the language of words
put it down to amnesia
and a kind of stammering.
I know better and at times
I can prove it in a look,
but usually I'm not constellated
so perfectly. On such occasions
JMW Turner diluted oils
with turpentine and used rags
to mark bare canvas up.
He too had to acquiesce
to the exigencies of a place
that deny silence is the matrix
of sound, the page a decoy
for what is really going on.
Only Aunt Dorothy understood
I would speak reluctantly
if at all, considering how dangerous
speech is, how ignorant, or maybe
demeaning's a better word,
and she died young,
taking with her my last chance
of getting by.
I couldn't bear to look
at the little model boat
she gave me, compass embedded
in its polished deck.
I've sailed by that compass
the north seas of malaise
and know it will burst into fire
when I die, like my will to speak.
So don't trouble me with words,
don't be afraid to look.

a decoy for what is really going on 4

Is it deathward not to like water
or only a matter of taste?
Shouldn't I celebrate water
in remembrance of life as a roach?
And if it's death to gulp the sea
why do I dream of it?
Perhaps because life is the moment we do it
or perhaps it's in mimicry
of having made other mistakes
with a determination so fierce
as to survive deserts and oceans
as utterances of dust.

I'd like to trade the relevance of this
for the inconsequence of that
in the hope of making sense
under a yellow lamplight in a park,
sense of this breathing of hatred upon
people already suffocating in shit,
but I'd have to know much more
than I do about fear, and I already know
too much to sleep or breathe regularly,
too much to hope for more than snow
to cover up the details of our choices.
I'm the active ingredient,
but who pours, stirs, whirls,
administers? Angels? I thought
they're witnesses, not meddlers.
Must I do everything? I always have.
I have no permission to tire, so, as usual,
each word's an outlaw, each thought a crime.

life is the moment we do it 6

Whatever it is I'm not resigned,
I'm centrifugally wed to flux,
not happy but content to blend
with uncertainties around me,
at times elixir or alembic,
above all aware, aware, obliged
to seize opportunities however
ridiculously they're offered me.
I didn't come by this conviction
thanks to privilege or luck, it took
eight decades of calamity
slogging to this state of grace.
I'd say now lettest thy servant depart,
but the only thing that's up to me
is to witness how hard is prayer.
I was born a glitch and had to make
an algorithm of myself and then
another one, until I aspired
to be a prick in the veil of illusion.
At that point all bets were off,
the wind rose, the weave unraveled,
I had no idea who the hell I was,
no further use for me, but someone
might and that, that felt good.

born a glitch,
a prick in the veil of illusion

The blessings of an anonymous face
are manifold, its prospects bleak.
It slides off mirrors and hopes to be
a paperclip lost in a carpet.
Some eyes fall lightly on us, some
feel us up. Spies
learn not to shed much of themselves,
to leave as little DNA as possible—
no scorch-trails on the floor, no
tricking up our furniture, no
watermarks on memory.
The memorable, searing face
must learn to ground lightning
to its keel, learn
to shudder secretly and soak up
encounters like sweat in the eye,
but an anonymous face gets by
like banter and dry dew.
We're not yet drowned in someone's wake,
sentient jetsam jettisoned
so that others could go on,
corked messages bobbing,
urgency's leavings, comings
lost in goings on,
what're-we's winking
among spilt diamonds, costs
of our faces, prices
of what we set eyes upon.

What's your name, boy?
Do I have to tell you?
Pieces of him keep falling off
until he's a wisp
of what he thinks he is,
a kind of glory.
An alleluia knocks
gargoyles from their perches
and in that flutter and scuttle
he slips under the door,
leaves the church to its squabbles,
leaves evidence of himself
to confound the crime scene squad.
Fuck you and your questions,
fuck his meaningless name,
he was never a consequence
and only because he remembered that
his pieces would not stay glued
until finally he gave them consent
to go be their many wonts
and they took him with them.
What's your name, boy?
Missing moment, call me that,
or any goddamn thing you want.
I stole your candy, your baseball cards,
but I left your daughter
for assholes with names.
Pieces of him keep falling off,
he can't keep it together,
which is altogether appropriate since
no one knows what it is.

I never looked like I should,
never looked as I should,
should never have looked at all
the heists I see in the mirror,
testimony of conflicting witnesses,
eye shadow of betrayals, caravans
along the silk roads of compliance,
encounters on the Danube, rape,
desertion, those certain truths
that bite the face like acid
until fume arises that can't be taken for
other than the bitterly wry
waving of doctors and lawyers away.
Never looked as if I'd brought
myself along to see this country
where every detail belongs so well
our clamor to belong offends
almost as much as my face
offends the mirror and seems
something I grabbed mistakenly
in a rush to meet a deadline,
deadline after which what,
deadline to accomplish what,
open which door, say which words,
take which direction, swing
which compass? And if I knew
the answers to these squalls
of exasperation, would I look
like the creature I left behind,
could I bear to look, or do you suppose
that once when I was a boy I did
and now am what's left?

Our looks are what we have to pay
for looking the other way
instead of changing course.
Stuck with them we pretend we didn't see
cracks in the surfaces of eventuality.
We rely on time to march us
to our execution date
when we should have prized the seam
of what we saw,
let the new dimension yaw
and be ourselves its consequence.
Our looks and the way we look
mesh, it's up to us
to unchain them or be snapped in two,
plastered on the wall
of stubbornness.
Hold on to your faces, hold on,
winds are gathering off West Africa,
blackboards are meant to be scrubbed.
Nail down these places, shut them up,
you've hid behind them long enough,
lying like presidents
about all they do for you.

Steamy window filled with friendly ladies
whose names and stories he can't remember
waves at him as he stands outside focusing
his camera on an abandoned church.
Pleased and annoyed, he nods and grins:
hasn't his life been like this, people
he half remembers, troubling redolence?
There they are at Baba Louie's partying,
distracting him. Here he is at a loss,
not lost but getting there, wishing
he could be more with it whatever it is,
knowing he's never known what it is
or where he'd be if he were there, and so
he waves as if he knows them, wondering
what his camera calmed, what it got,
thinking we're beset with so much detail
where we stand we're beside ourselves.
Is that where we ought to be or should
we smile behind a steamy window waving
at a bill cap turned backwards on a man
who seems to have come into his own?

beset with so much detail

It could have been avoided if he hadn't stared,
hadn't tipped the suspect off, the suspect
suspected of not being one of us,
but now the girl with the dissolving mouth
fills the emergency room with silence
and the only crisis then is noise,
sirens and klaxons of self-importance,
backing beeps and monotone alarms
of pretending to know what's going on
in a world a fey girl's glance can quash.
And it does. The room turns much too white
all because he stared, had to have,
insisted on having that little space
he needed to perform a sacred rite,
which was none of anyone's business
until he had to give it a name,
demand an address and numbers,
assert an insufferable self
where there was blessed none.

    hold on to your faces, hold on

We didn't what we didn't
and this is the consequence of that,
thunder murmuring on a mesa,
glimpsing each other in passing cars,
skittering across a drafty floor,
didn't, arguing that we couldn't,
knowing that we should have,
singing countertenor in our bones,
sickening us in our settlements.
The occasions we didn't rise to
are now the malarias of our ways.
We are what we didn't as much as
what we did. Our night vision
which ought to be failing falls
on antlered creatures summoning us
when we thought witness could be denied.
Dying is to be strung like Manhattan
by its 21 harps and played
by the fingers we clothe ourselves against,
to be wind-whipped, shredded,
made over, sung to pieces, begun
uncertain of what is done.

We shouldn't eat, it's vulgar.
Rainwater and starlight
ought to be enough,
we ought to be fey
and dance between the beams
of each other's eyes,
we ought to salvage dignity
and be androgynous
instead of cadging sex,
and yet these oughts, they too
disgrace us. Come, let's bathe
in hails of ancient light,
scrub off our DNA and wait
for our lost selves to catch up.

played by the fingers we clothe ourselves against

singing countertenor in our bones
waiting for the crystal ship to arrive

All this living by dumbfounding rules,
drink after work, darknesses
not so much architectural as
the shadows of our breasts, the longing
for significance that stops
the crevasses between us with dread.
The commute is much too long
between childhood and this
accommodation, this emergency
called for lack of a better word
our youth, our compromise.
How can we challenge this in the WC
and emerge relieved of the urgency
of playing at this, pretending that?
What a laugh, that gender-neutral sign
in this unneutral place.
How can we return to the bar
something like the kid who saw it straight,
whatever it was or claimed to be,
how can we say no and think
beyond Verrazano Narrows,
beyond the bell buoys, horns and sirens,
to the port and starboard uncertainties
of a decent life among the whales?
From the garments and makeup of tomorrow,
the dismantlements of tonight,
the rocking subways of our despair,
Good Lord deliver us.
From the syrupy sycophancy,
the feeling up and knocking down
and getting over on,
surrenders of our wilding selves,

wake us, make us Saint Elmo's Fire,
green flash in the riggings of commerce,
lightning at dusk, boisterous journey.
Anything, not this, not this bitter trek
back from the WC to the bar.

Were we where our DNA has been?
Depends on who we are,
leavings on toilet seats, worn-out parts,
pee on the floor,
or a particular song whose harmonics
do work we assign them
in a smile that brushes the face
of a stranger a hundred years ahead.
Were we there, assuming we know
where there is and who we are,
or did we give a spare identity away,
leaving something yellow in a waste basket,
an identity we declared surplus,
excess not lost but left
because it was the only way
to slip the reflection in the pond
that guards its terrible holiness,
to slip behind the doppelganger
in the mirror, to erase the silver cynic
that deceives us in the morning.
Where were we when we thought
we were some place familiar,
slippery as it was,
and where are we now but in the space
we need to conceive of ourselves
as so much more than we've ever been?

Not in some guttering dream
or in my imagination
but in an unhitched stare
I saw her overlooking France,
Brooklyn at her feet.
She was smiling as if she knew
that one thing, that secret
reserved for each of us not to know.
The bridge became her harp,
even though she was not a blonde,
but that was just the point,
nothing was as it should have been
and that's how I knew I couldn't be dead
although it had been said of me,
couldn't be dead because I'd seen her
not as I stood in this puddle
but in a time when appearances had changed,
a time where I belonged more than here.

not in some guttering dream

I hope for an unimaginable species,
beings I need epiphanies to describe,
but every word's a sin against truth,
every line a struggle to be honest.
Defeat must be welcomed,
as every artist knows, and bitterness
of a kind that blesses apples
cinnamoned to humble us, help us understand
we are not the ultimate of anything,
but interim creatures, intervals
run rampant in an interlude,
disrespectful, angry to be mortal.
The best we can do is open our arms
at night to the species coming in.

41

Brooklyn at her feet

Damned if I know, can't get inside,
too gloomy there anyway,
inside the marrow where I'd know
why I was born to be kept out,
for having no neighborhood in spite
of lukewarm cordialities,
for being the one to get away from
and witnessing it all denied
in the name of also doing business as
human beings, damned if I know
if this isn't inside out
and I've lived upside down
and inside is out and I'm an angel
whose wings encompass it all,
damned if I know and not knowing is
a benediction not unlike a grain of sand
or the salt content of a gram of sea
or seeing too much to bother finally
to be a member of a clan
or anything so demeaning.
I don't believe it for a minute,
arch palaver of the Sunday social club,
the Monday walk-around as truth,
predatory truth of savages in suits,
ill-suited to be herbivores.
I don't believe we suffer the children,
we suffer them not at all,
and they suffer us until
they too become insufferable,
sociable, smarmy, alarming
to creatures still intact,
damned but at least awake.

arch palaver of the Sunday social clubs

Doubt I'll sleep through a night again,
but I slip through keyholes
fondling tumblers as I pass,
mindful time is not a sprint
but a passage checked
only by illusions, hampered
only by possessions, harried
only by ourselves. Doubt
I loiter here but to remember this,
so I ought to be grateful
never to have belonged
and to have longed not as much.

He's seriously ill of seeing too much,
juniper goosing spruce, grimace
of disuse, digitalia behaving acridly,
serial abuse of dandelions and children,
seriously ill of reading what's unsaid,
of being unable to filter dissonance
out of seemingly sociable rooms

creatures still intact,
damned but at least awake

Do you know this salvage tug's name?
Call it anything I've ever been called,
lumbering groan and grimace
out of Rotterdam where diamonds
are cut, fortunes made parsing greed,
call it salvor of scuttled memories
pounding back to my crib, ploughing
through high seas of spoilage, divers
playing cards below, deckhands
sorting gear, radio crackling,
Nosferatu lighting a screen
like approaching ships, seriously ill
of having to do this again to regain
a semblance of balance to go on, and on
to what but eventually going down
far below the reach of card players
or even their robot submarines, below
the level of all understanding to the deep
knowledge that whatever it was for
it is done and now lies under silt
hiding a hint of ennoblement.

God looks out from certain faces
wordless as an onanym. I'll explain.
But if not others', it's not God.
No, you must understand
it's a matter of readiness
to bear witness, to see
the unspoken word, a truth
that rests in reticence,
a thought undecided
what to become.

It happened on Third Avenue
outside the Russian clockmaker's,
this encounter of an old man
with blue numbers on his arm
and a man called Individual 1,
a prime actor in this moment,
an elixir dropped into a vial,
a whiff of transcendence,
rising like smoke from Auschwitz.

The cost of belonging is too high,
that's what the old man's pleading look
would have the younger man undo,
undo the payment of an exorbitant price
for the delusions of the tribe?
Or does it say rescue me
for turning away from the abyss,
rescue me for surviving this
when in our grand compulsion to look in
we're glorious even if
society exists to call it sin?
Is this what he's called to do
one bright afternoon on Third Avenue,
rescue the turned-away from a mistake,
ask them at the weakest point
to stare at what they spurned?
He stutters. The old man reaches up
and holds his face in his hands.
You are God, no use denying it.
And in that great din he hears
the clockmaker's clocks ticking,
every one, even the unrepaired.

Nothing I have to say to you
goes down like oysters and Sancerre.
It all comes out asparagus pee
as if something had gone wrong,
untrustworthy plumbing,
sulfur whiff of rotten eggs,
not to be believed because
its virgin note rang true.

You are God,
no use denying it

What lacks in all of this
is that essential this-ness that
electrifies a room,
something so personal
it summons sobs, urgency
that changes colors
and, you could swear,
subtly rearranges things.
I should be fully here,
a bona fide inhabitant,
instead I am a remnant,
blueness under Luminol,
something left, revenant
apologetic yet dangerous,
not someone you can trust
yet entrusted with the place.
God help us all, but
in this roaring absence,
playing God, we presume
to know too much, simultaneously
feigning ignorance, a feat
we call civilization,
savage word.

savage word
goes down like oysters and Sancerre

I cleaned that Cycladian face with steel wool,
erasing microbial empires, but when I passed
over where eyes might have been I saw
faces I'd known in half-forgotten lives.
Number Four steel wool rubs fingerprints
off museum glass, traces of handling.
Eyelessly ungrateful for my attention, that face,
as ungrateful as I've been for caretakers
who took too much care in the middle of the night.
I understood. I was grateful to understand
I had merely interfered with the greater work
of gods who grant all we don't need to see
with such poor excuses for eyes, all
we don't need to eat to thrive, and
the forty thousand scents we need to identify
what's really going on to stay alive.
I pulled wool over their absent eyes
in a fit of telling myself convenient lies.

as ungrateful as I've been for caretakers
and convenient lies

Disgrace, disgrace to want to get in
or want to be one side of a wall.
Grandeur to long to be all,
glory to belong to none.

Should we rise in one last heroic feat
to move to an apartment by the sea,
beg buoy gongs absolve us of the dappled mania
of hard looks, extorted smiles & radiances
too sharp to bear, the summer of hard looks?
Come to the theater, look at the back of heads
and ask yourself if it's worth it, this disguise
of savagery, the flashing scalpels of summer
tearing us apart, remorseless as naked legs
and beauty that mocks winter's wisdom?
Is it worth it to crane around these heads
to vet the sweating dancers, to see if
they see us, to see what we saw in the crib
and let our parents talk us out of it?
Worth what? What price would we exact
if we could see? A moving van,
considerate helpers, a week of zest,
to watch the fog roll in, gulls wheel,
whales leap, a last vacation
from the macrons, breves, mainline enders
of this murderous shebang, this tinkering
of cracked pots leaking epiphanies.
Summer of raptor beaks and razor blades,
reptilian interrogations, fetid nakedness
more fearful than brazen, summer glittering
in a confabulation of memories as close
to transfiguration as we get, memories
sculpting, not redacting or censoring,
unsatisfied with themselves, discontent
with their encampments in our minds.

I've always been too respectful to feel at home
or to travel much, wary of being a rummager,
a rapist even, more inclined to read my way
to other places, especially between the lines.
My shoes don't fit, my passport's fake,
my documents have been seized, my eyes
detect strangers' SS underwear, my ears
hear untoward argot beneath the warble
of ordinary discourse. One last heroic effort
to founder on the beach, to grin
like cast-up sharks poked by children,
that might do, but summer closes in,
cocoons and fungi shroud bright leaves,
cataracts clouding sight, dimming
prospects of bluffing one more checkpoint.

Come to the theater, look at the backs of heads

I don't remember what it was like to be 13,
or 33, not this accordion, this fold-up,
fold-out, fade-in, fade-out gewgaw.
I don't remember what it was like
to be anything but a wonderment
and a work of part-time despair,
but sometime I see it hanging in trees
at dusk, what I was like,
not in months or years but moments
that still make my nostrils flare,
moments that went down well
or came back up too fast, doodads
of a time of artifice, artifacts
up from the debris fields of my mind,
not Christmas ornaments, but twigs
snapped for trackers, tatters left
for those brave enough
to recollect, to relive the dismay
of children undressed in the dark
of the wounded's hard purposes.
I don't remember what it was like.
I've had to find context, to make it
out of broken pieces, broken from me,
broken by me, pieces unlike the bays
and peninsulas of puzzle parts,
smoothed out by lies, bent, warped,
and what I've made is continents
in search of civilizations to host.
That is my accomplishment,
and it deserves to be nameless,
it has earned its nakedness, its contempt
for the fear inherent in identity.

Dandelions bode well for potatoes.
I've harvested all kinds of tubers—
radishes, carrots, turnips, parsnips, beets,
intentions.
Sandy soil is best for these sacrifices.
They're not like poison ivy, oak, ash,
all the pretentious lovelies, not
invasive, they're Aztec blood-debts,
deserving bent knees, devout hands.
I understand the landed, sinuously rooted,
possessive—envied, loathed and loved them,
but we're not for each other. They yearn
to fill a canvas, they don't get Cézanne.
They're stranger-makers, customs officials,
unlike the warm and yielding sand
where I harvested potatoes drunk
on briny Great South Bay. Dandelions
frighten developers and lawyers.
Invasive, as I said, they mistake
metastasis for growth they insist is good,
and when they're finally cut up and harvested
they whinge and haunt under moldy stones.
I'm a keen observer of them, but all they've seen
of me is foreignness, enough
to foreclose on properties,
proprieties, decencies and me, enough
to set out flags and yellow ribbons and set off
fireworks to celebrate their deep roots
rotting in polluted soil, a keen observer,
mourner, advocate, student of all
they are so perfect at making strange.

> *should we rise in one last heroic feat*
> *to leave some canvas blank*

54

Summer of hard looks, station breaks,
weather breaks, failed brakes of days hurtling
towards one last recognition too hard to bear,
that epiphany that hurls us with it
into Saint Catherine's ecstatic mouth.

Heart, don't beat—lungs, don't fill,
not until that perfect moment arrives
when your forlorn wish overshadows
the decent man you might have become
had you not gone cryogenic waiting
for something glamorous.
That something that's supposed to happen
is you becoming you opposed
to flighty imaginings and shit
your parents fed you, the line you bought
to get along, the go-along psychosis
of nationalists and rub-a dub-dub chumminess
that puts civilizations on the clock
and tells them when it's time to come down.

> *rub-a-dub-dub chumminess*
> *tells them when it's time to come down*

Clouds growl, gutters drip, frogs gronk,
Venus shies, barns combust, sirens wail,
but none of it removes the snags we set
before our feet, the mold that clasps
our sculpted stories. None of it parses
as we wait for lightning to illuminate
creatures gathering beyond this weir,
none of it reassures us we're provident
enough not to trip on suppositions
we've lined up in our way, not to break
our necks falling down familiar stairs.

In this SCIF of winking motherboards,
this electronic galaxy, life consists
of *us-be-me's*. Part the cheeks
of secrecy, lick the goo of seals
not meant to hold, stick your tongue
between the yaw of signaling stars,
resent the caginess of environments,
pray to be whole and not a particle
pulled into holes, knowing how forlorn
it is to be contained, poured out
into vessels that make us vassals
doomed to reach, not to be reached,
breached, patched, scarred over,
furious to be partitioned, pigeonholed.

forlorn to be contained

We claw, we yearn, we knock outside   35
the wood, the bone, the steel, the flesh
presumed to harbor hearth—
our presumption overpowers us,
and when they invented container ships
little did they see them as a metaphor
for the evil of insiderdom, wiles
that make outsiders of us all, outsiders
desperate to keep others out,
to poke the coals of specialness,
to challenge the papers of the suspect,
man the checkpoints between
here and there, belonging and foreignness,
names, imprisoning, namelessness
a benediction that flirts with death.

    summer of hard looks, station breaks
    desperate to keep others out

Disgrace, disgrace to want to get in
or want to be one side of a wall.
Grandeur to long to be all,
glory to belong to none.

Certain faces look in on us
from dim times to this
for reasons we have not lived long enough
to understand, look over at us from behind counters,
through the cross-currents of crowds,
from doorways,
passing cars, corners, solemnly as if
the moment had finally arrived when
that one friendship is reborn that defines
what we've glimpsed through rain,
the downpour of events, flash floods of dismay.
Certain faces look in on us remembering
everything we've set aside,
not with pity or impatience but sorrow
that expects us to have wings,
and I think if we dare look back we do.

We are each other's collaborative projects,
that's the physics of it in spite of our arrogance,
and all our individualism is charade, trappings
to deny we can't breathe without ruffling
foreigners' skin, just as the butterfly in Szechuan
ripples the puddle in Schenectady.
But it's a solemn matter to conceal
such knowledge with our lives
because the duty it imposes is too great
for all but the maddest of us to bear.

Disgrace to deny such common knowledge,
to brush over our parents' tracks
as if we owe them a debt for baffling us.

Deliver us from our terrible intuitions,
deliver us from asking, deliver us
from the delights of playing dumb,
its hollow comfort, the emptiness
of thinking ourselves native to a place,
of hiding behind a convenient face,
a clump of data, a conviction in blood
that turns us into animated mud.

Deliver us from our dread identities, 40
inspire us to respect the circle
that represents what we don't know,
move us to ask whether
enigmas are nothing but the weather
of the circle, its atmosphere.

our dread identities
turn us into animated mud

They make that eerie sound in horror flicks—
banshee instrument, waterphone,
song of that glimpse that makes life sham.
You get this, you get Dorian Gray.
That picture in the attic is as much a con
as our presentable selves,
considering the muck in which we're stuck.
We're always straining to hear above the noise
of what goes on,
the weeping afterwards,
rubbing the ineradicable sob,
gasping, remembering something
in a stranger's face, puking of it,
dying of it, what we call Amityville
and its sequels, but we know the worst
is yet to come, which is why we're never able
to take those deep breaths we're ordered to,
never able to undress again unwary,
because we ourselves are that instrument,
locked in the room where it happened,
it being that one thing
that seeks to use life as cover-up,
that buries itself in events.

> *grandeur to long to be all,*
> *banshee instrument*
> *ineradicable sob*

I am a mud boy, it took rain
or at least piss to make me.
Two European women and a Bedouin boy
slung mud at each other in Bou Saada
from which I took shape in Algiers.
In Ouargla the temperature was 120.
Camus was finishing his studies in Algiers
that summer I popped from a gamester's womb,
the stirring of a puddle by butterfly wings.
Lucky for them they now had me
to vex them and more to do
than they had time to stew.
There wasn't much hope of rain,
a pissing match would have to do.
Mud boy could not be made to cry,
or suck, so it was decided,
after they'd cleaned themselves up,
he would be a golem.
Nudge the little pawn with a forefinger,
play the knight, the queen,
the bishop and the rook.

> *I am a mud boy, it took rain*
> *Or at least piss to make me*

Forgetting what to do next is homage
not rehearsal for what is to come.

I made a lame run at it.
All manner of beasts stood in the way.
What was it other than
the quietude so many thought
ought to be shaken out of me?
He's listening too carefully,
observing too much, they thought.
I've run past them now,

gone behind the moon, leaving
a snapshot of a boy holding his nanny's hand
beside a Breyer's ice cream cart
as the evening primrose opens
in trembling Brooklyn.

Years thunder over me.

I squirrel in a ditch, pull bramble up.
I'm not cowering, I'm braiding wild carrot lace
into a fragrant crown, I croak with the frogs,
honk with herons, keck with redwings,
swamp gas in this interregnum waiting
for the years to adjust themselves according
to an algorithm I understood when I arrived
but left in a taxicab
or dropped over the rails of *Saturnia*.
I don't know, but it will come back to me,
I'll recover it and get up and look around
as if I'm not nearsighted and confused
and have always been able to carry a tune.

Disgrace, disgrace to want to get in
or want to be one side of a wall.
Grandeur to long to be all,
glory to belong to none.

Disgrace to deny such common knowledge,   45
to brush over our parents' tracks
as if we owe them a debt for baffling us.

homage, not rehearsal
I croak with the frogs

Jehlool da ghoul doesn't need a name,
he'd rather be one of the numberless glints
of an unhurried wave, a holy spook
inhabiting glades & forbidden creases,
moistening under silk, whooshing the wheat
of thighs, ashamed to be an entity,
anything contained or categorized.

Too bad he didn't know the nature of his guilt,
mistook his light for darkness,
but he can't be said to have wasted time,
having imagined this for himself,
shedding needs to cap his ghoulish career.
Jehlool da ghoul would rather stain a cheek
or fill a navel basin with a fleet of cheers
or contrive an unmentionable scent
than be handed over the heads of fools.

Never mind what others say of what others said,
Da ghoul knows what it's like to be dead.

The coat and cap on the hook
are merely where I've been,
symbolic, remnant more elegant than me,
relaxed and unbespoken,
indifferent to intent, watchful
if seemingly unwary, as I was
during my service in mufti.
Much as they reek of me
I'm fading under the gaze
of strangers passing by the window.
There was never a chance

of retaining my colors,
but here I listen to music,
hear the toilet flush,
neighbors quarreling.
I was never good at hanging around
and I'm no more trusted here
than in my bilious shape,
but I'm as overlooked
as carillons & inshallahs.

Nudge the little pawn with a forefinger
play the knight, the queen,
the bishop and the rook.

Bullheaded, the town refused
to remove the death trap at Cemetery
& County 8, a stone wall that outlived
its usefulness and now sent drivers
into harm's way like children
exiled from the warmth of denial
in fimbulwinter of 18th birthdays.
Who does the town wish to kill,
the tax assessor or the stranger
whose credit's more welcome than him?
Someone's ready for the good ole boys
to mop up and cart away, native,
immigrant, quarterback, cheerleader,
does it matter as long as the stone wall wins?
Blame DC for anything of consequence,
not the nativists at the firehouse
who hate newcomers almost as much
as those whose skins shout the other,
tie yellow ribbons on sick trees
the town treats as foreigners.
The slightest whiff of difference,
a wish more cancerous than pesticide,
cheaper, courteous, shrewd.

who does the town wish to kill?

What's your background, may I ask?
I'd rather talk about unseen foreground,
details sacrificed to noisy color
or perhaps the underground into which
the city's sinking as we speak, but you,
I understand, want me to be my data
rather than to share what epiphanies
might come of studying our reflections
in the pupils of each other's eyes.

    the city's sinking as we speak

My hair sweeps forward in the manner
of Augustus on my left and back
in the manner of Stalin on my right.
I am an ultracentrifuge parsing particles
from mirage and illusion.
If you're cockeyed looking at me
it's because I'm parting your tale
from its moral, spinning something
out of control to study it
at such breakneck speed
as never to get my name right
all for the purpose of never believing
a damned thing you say.
Such men cannot be buried,
they whirl up out of the grave,
they must be burned and laid,
fed to the rats of U Thant Island
from the secretary-general's house,
put out at night like garbage,
unplugged unceremoniously,
peed out to avoid an accident.
Beware such men in their baseball caps.
Here's what you must not do:
you must not avoid their gaze
or it will follow you.

fed to the rats of U Thant Island
such men cannot be buried

Rest not in peace but centrifugal turmoil,
particles of glee, gloom and harmony,
Mevlevis whirling arms outstretched,
not oppressed by earth but separated
from compromises such as name and category,
entranced by selflessness, swirling,
lives reconstituting themselves, not in peace,
not crazed, but quintessentials returning
to wholenesses sometimes glimpsed in art.
Not some harmless gaffer in a baseball cap,
not unless your eyes never clarified,
but a grinning centrifuge come to terms
with the deathliness of peace and quiet,
their lack of inspiration, harmful crone
set on molesting bad ideas, committing crimes
against a state of being stuck in root,
soil, blood, clan, tribe, rags and ideologies.

I'm parting your tale from its moral
molesting bad ideas

Call the person who was never there

your hollowness who ought to have been there,
who disturbs curtains in no breeze
and moves you to weep unexpectedly
for no reason except the conviction
people pass through you on their way
to assignations compared to which
you're hardly a blade of grass—
call that person
the sigh that ripples your startled hair
on an August day too hot to breathe.
You assumed once too often that fable
was there as a familiar face and you knew
where there is when in fact it is
a useless all-purpose wrench sold
by a pricey store to such sad fools
as you were until this still day.

> *you're hardly a blade of grass*
> *a useless all-purpose wrench*

He swings his head away from you
and yet looks you in the eye
as if to say goodbye
while telling his life story.
Your look holds his balance
in its sway even if you don't want
the responsibility, and in that way
you're indebted to each other,
but what is really going on?
Has brain-cargo shipped
from port to starboard
so that he must swing his rudder
to the high sea of your intent?
What do you make of this?
It's an afterimage after all—
decades have passed
since you sat across from him wondering
if your face was too bright to bear,
your gaze a glare, if he wanted something
you were not prepared to give
or if perhaps he simply failed
to say what was on his mind,
a few words that might have launched
you like a paper plane out the window
into the Cordoban courtyard
of someone else's dreams.
Why couldn't he finish,
why couldn't you drew it out of him,
that simple desire to be friends?
It wasn't because you crossed your legs
or because of the tic of an eyelid,
it wasn't because your smile fled
and a shadow crossed your face,
it was because he suddenly knew

he mistook your innocence for guile,
how incapable of apologizing he was,
how incapable you were of imagining
decency flummoxed him.

   it wasn't because you crossed your legs

I'm no known instrument,
but I've been played by otherlings.
Occasionally I hear their names for me,
but I don't remember them when I wake,
only that I heard them
and we shared fits of delight.
I may have started as an oud,
intimate, innocent, and wound up
as a pipe organ in a leaky cathedral
or a waterphone in the woods.
I may have been an harmonica
or a flute, but I imagine myself
as a note not quite struck,
a dangerous loiterer summoned
by creatures at the edge of the bog,
the ones I saw when I was being raped
in a school that existed for my own good,
the ones I see when auras don't get in the way.
Sometimes, sometimes I see them
part auras as if they're cobwebs.
I exist to stare them in the face,
oud or organ, witting or unwitting,
I exist for that moment
whenever it opens for me,
and as it is now, as I pile blankets on,
I feel their piquant warmth approach.

> *started as an oud,*
> *been an harmonica or a flute*

In old age I'm a raven alarmed
by every secret tic, alert
to the tremor of an eye,
to the sigh of pubic hair,
extreme in all aspects except
doing anything about it—
in that I'm still a boughten child, numb
in the cold clamp of denial.
I know it's better to be shot in office
than rally the base instinct
that always tripped me up
in the eleventh hour. I know
I don't have to rock the liturgy
going on below. I can fly out
the clerestory window,
a proper raven, and shit
on someone's kid.
Something should be settled
if I unwrinkle tinfoil, hit
woodpeckers with tennis balls,
take pictures of reflections
in puddles, but instead
promises stink of molesters
and rip my hemorrhoids.
I ought to welcome this as evidence
I amount to something in spite
of my preternatural stare,
but I walk in the valley of the shadow
of a certain young widow's tit
without papers, without rights,
barely able to hold on
to my uncertain name.

   walk in the valley of the shadow
   of a certain young widow's tit

Purge this old crock of its gassy vileness,
shut the laboratory down, let ghosts take over,
vines throttle pretension. Darkness polishes
instruments used for bad purposes,
polish them now for angels, rid
them of aspirations, come, ennoblers
out of the trees now that lightning
makes microscopes of your eyes, come
trace your fingers over this old retort
as if you knew how to use it once
somewhere on the Persian Gulf
in the service of some old coot, claiming
you would turn lead to gold, growing
wings on the backs of the fallen.

   trace your fingers over this old retort

Heaven but for the snippy waitresses,
ticks in the high grass
and the usual exhibitionists.
Heaven but for having the runs
and remembering I didn't get any medals
for my particular disabilities
or for keeping my mouth shut.
Heaven, clouds hurrying out of Canada
and davening the fields of Ghent,
heaven, this sculpture park
with its steles and totems
and inscriptions like no trespass signs.

    Heaven but for my distrust of words,
    snippy waitresses and exhibitionists

Picking up a paper in a vanished room 57
and finding sanctuary under tablecloths,
is the same as doing it now, depending
on which hallway my mind is haunting,
which face you happen to be wearing,
the temperature of your brow, the choice
you make and now wish to undo, the paper's
disposition in the moonlight filtering in,
the sunlight threatening some new horror
or perhaps the grandeur of saying nothing
in light of what wants to unfold, in spite
of the wonts of armed and loitering ghouls.
Picking up a paper in that vanished room
is more hazardous than killing Bin Laden,
it's the subject of angels' songs, the glisten
of clitoral rose windows, the invitation
of choral labia to the sanctuary
where linear time is a B-movie, the script
whatever's lugged to the altar innocently.

picking up a paper in a vanished room
finding sanctuary under tablecloths

58

Then I'd have to hang my lungs
on a steel tree and roll them around
among darting ghosts. My heart
I'd leave in a mess of read-outs.
I'd look for words under stickums,
smile bleakly at orderlies, aim
for the bloody sun at the end
of the hall which I'd now perceive
as having been my life. But
I didn't have to do these things
because Antarctica melted,
the oceans rose 180 feet
and Brooklyn Bridge became
a buoy picket. Did I really live
that long? I think I did. I think
we know so little about time
and strangers who look like us
that this hall which I've painted
as a hospital may be a tunnel
through which my lives pass
in all their various dreams,
door to door, hurriedly as if
they must catch up with someone
who has gone ahead and signals
from a clearing in which none
of this is quite as real or urgent
as what's ahead. Good morning,
Miss What's Your Name, yes,
that's exactly where I'm going
and won't need to breathe
or listen to that damned drum,
exactly what I've become.

Antarctica melted,
the oceans rose 180 feet

Lost in this blubbery room
unlit but for my mind.
No words paint its slathery sides.
What happens if
I prong that black hole there?
Is there virtue in
being other than outside?
Is this the opposite of other,
having been swallowed,
not yet digested?
What is the nature of the whole,
what metaphors, analogies
suffice? I said lost,
I could have said found
and felt no better
but for the warmth of my mind.
That bicycle there,
I see its chain's woven
of holy recognitions, are they mine?
Beyond the pale
the wavering streets groan with their secrets.
I've found the station I was supposed to find,
boarded up and yet inviting,
and put my luggage down to climb a hill
where eagles tend each other
and have forgotten to prey,
forgotten or forgone as I forgo
magazine urgencies,
what I was taught to need, and sleep,
but first I must stop lying like presidents,
relish homeliness,
cherish dismay,

and smilingly make
no attempt to recover my luggage.
None. No one. Not one.

Is this the opposite of other,
what is the nature of the whole?

We got a little tired towards the end,   60
slept in the cusps of wildflowers
as they spun downstream, dreamed
of strange cities where we'd been
in the half-remembered light of lives
we seemed to have been living while
walking hand in hand here on earth.
And we had to get reacquainted,
each morning, reintroduced
by the nurses of the winter sun.
We became unfamiliar to ourselves,
dizzy watching branches overhead,
studying the arteries of cloud creatures.
We waited for the crystal ship to arrive,
occasionally laughing at the ferocity
of our assailants, the persistence
of mistaken identity, the presumption
of those who had insisted they knew us
and the difficulty of knowing ourselves.
More than a little tired but eager
to start out again as friends.

Selected Poems

2001-2019

FAR FROM ALGIERS

Poems by Djelloul Marbrook

Winner of the 2007 Stan and Tom Wick Poetry Prize
Ted Derricotte, Judge

2008, Kent State University Press, Ohio

The winner of the 2007 Stan and Tom Wick Poetry Prize and the 2010 International Book Award in poetry, *Far from Algiers* explores the poet's feelings of not belonging to family or country. When he was fourteen yeears old the poet began writing poems in Manhattan. In his thirties he abandoned poetry after publishing a few poems in small journals, but he never stopped reading and studying poetry. Then in 2001, appalled by the 9/11 terrorist attacks, the poet within awakened. Stuffing blue notebooks in his pockets, he began walking around Manhattan determined to affirm his beloved home in the wake of the attacks. *Far from Algiers* emerged from hundreds of poems he has composed in the years since. His voice speaks to all who've ever had doubts about belonging. Born in Algiers to an American artist and a Bedouin father and arriving in America as a dying infant, he has contemplated this issue throughout his life. *Far from Algiers* explores belonging in a society in denial about its own nativist sentiments. It speaks of the struggle to belong in a culture that pays lip service to assimilation but does not fully accept anyone perceived as foreign. Marbrook examines this issue with unflinching honesty.

Stuff the mailboxes and night repositories
against my attempts to insert
flat evidence of my belonging here.

I'm as sick of wanting to get in
as I am of wanting to be heard.
I was born with one of those faces that say

Trust me, you don't want to hear it.
Bad enough listening to myself,
who needs you to confirm the news?

My climate's not suitable for growing
the fruit expected of your tree
and I see you have no patience for experiment.

I've misunderstood great men in useful ways
in the natural course of an alien life,
so why would I quarrel with locked doors?

I don't know, djinni, how much you remember
but I know you measure the Sahara's sands,
wear stars on your fingers
and remember that once on Third Avenue
an old man freed you and asked nothing.
You studied him a long time before you left
to make sure he understood the consequences.
He did. And then he left,
and somewhere a child was born
wearing them on his face.

How do their flutes in the Tuareg night
summon us to the secrets of the djinn,
and how does the sexual electric of stars
wake us to the meanness of our wishes?
I think hearing is easier than seeing them
thanks to our brushes with the vast.
Abhor the misshapenness of words
and make this gnosis your heart:
everything is a facet of the same jewel.

And what is your background?
I have an advanced degree in bastardy.
Excuse me, I'm not familiar . . .
Of course you're not, there's no excuse.

I am a highly skilled outsider,
learned even. Nothing can shake me
from my resolve to leave
or my distrust of doors.

There is only my djinni to lead me
through the loud exhibitionism of the world.
Only my djinni affirms
groups are to keep us out.

Being born somebody's bastard
made me everyone's. I went
about the work of finding
the idea of belonging strange.

I am to the left of belonging,
forlorn, bereft and looking in.
Some are conceived under stars,
I was conceived under stairs.

You asked what my background is.
I wish I had one, but if I did
I would probably know less than I do
and be more certain about it.

When I reached the counter
the clerk looked behind me.

All a floor can be relied on
is to tip and turn to ice.

When I see familiar faces
they see someone else.

It's better to be invisible
than inconvenient,

the latter having no advantages.
I thought it would help to make reports,

but it seems that requires a home.
I was the least thing I'd forgotten.

No one waited for me,
no one regretted leaving,

but there were few regrets
I didn't manage to entertain.

My wake is smaller
than a periscope's.

Nothing ever happened
that couldn't without me.

Some would call it a Sufi life
if it had won their attention.

That's not what submarines do.

Real wars are fought at home;
historic wars reflect them.

I destroyed enough by accident;
I didn't need orders to confuse me.

What's hidden hums
from the back of things
behind boxes and faces,
low current in the seams
of stories we've hung up.

I dowse for resources
quickening in the dark.
Sucker punches bruise my heart
when I slip around to the back,

that's how I know I'm hot.
Everywhere there's facade
the street signs are turned around
and in such beguiling places.

True home is through enemy lines,
true enemies pose as friends.
Whoever's selling nothing
is a truly frightening man.
I hope you've met one lately.

It wasn't those who said they did
who had my good in mind.

Maybe I thought within a great within
were the grandeurs of the cosmos, or
one little secret might clothe me better
through thorny meetings I'd forgotten.

Success came cheap to those
who, looking after me, didn't look at all.
Who wished us less than freedom
gave us faith and apocalypse.

Threats of bad acting stopped
my too respectful mouth,
I knew I had a fatal crack;
I squirmed away from touch.

When I was young I didn't have the sort of face
men of consequence cotton to,
but the desolate studied me
in subway cars. I hear their heartbeats now
under the grates. I remember their faces.
I think I have kept faith with them,
but I would be hard put to tell them how.

The professors had a great deal to say,
saying nothing the desolate said more.
My bones were their tuning fork.

Then there were the inevitables
who lost themselves disliking me;
among them count lovers and my mother.
I think of them with a sob and permanent dismay.

The tribe inhabiting your face
remembers an ancient feud with me,
but its envoys pretend we've just met.

I would rather my own face teem
with the cities whose streets I've walked
and lovers who nurse no quarrels with me.

Somewhere between cliché and adage
and under a foot of snow
I fell down, cried and froze to death.

It was one thing to hear lightning
break off the past, another
to think I'd never see it again.

Heaven didn't interest me very much;
I was trying to imagine a place
where there would be nothing to say,

no getting lost or loss.
It was better than soiled fantasy
even if I had to start to finish.

If they don't file me in that truck,
if I only rest, I'm glad the snow has covered
the backwardness of my going forth.

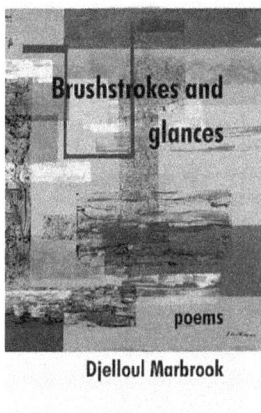

2010, Deerbrook Editions, Maine

"... looks at art the way a drinker drinks—deeply, passionately, and desperately, as if his life depended on it ... you want to run out to your favorite museum and look again, as you have never looked before, until the lights go out."

—Barbara Louise Ungar, author of *Immortal Medusa, Thrift, The Origin of the Milky Way* & *Charlotte Brontë, You Ruined My Life*

"... the poems here about museums, galleries, and studios are as penetrating as the ones about the art ... testify to years of careful seeing."

—Maggie Anderson, founding editor of the Wick Poetry First Book Series and the Wick Poetry Chapbook Series for Ohio Poets; author of *Dear All, Windfall: New and Selected Poems, A Space Filled with Moving, Cold Comfort, Years That Answer, Greatest Hits: 1984-2004* & *The Great Horned Owl*

"... one of those colossal poets able to bridge worlds— poetry and art, heart and mind—with rare wit, grace, and sincerity ..."

—Michael Meyerhofer, author of *Leaving Iowa, Blue Collar Eulogies* and *Damnatio Memoriae*

(The Brooklyn Museum)

May I stay here in diorite
a millennium or two,
chat amiably with Thoth
or Horus, worry
about Ra and Apophis
but not Ponzi schemes?

I'd like to be a shabti
awakened at night
by Nefertiti
to prepare her bath
and anoint her with oil,
to rest in a cedar box

and not think of news,
to be an amulet,
a cylinder resting
between Isis's breasts.
I'd like to stay here
when the lights go out.

Painter of undersides of leaves,
shuddered cubist light, Corot
held seconds in his hands,
listening to their murmurings.

Aspens were his populace.
Conspiring with their haste to go,
he daubed their babbling whispers
with scents of sisters fled.

The cool nostalgias of your genes
confide Corot is your native due.
Before you came as hostages here
you were notes struck upon the air.

She can hardly touch herself
much less bear others' touch
whose groping looks rummage
the secret loving in her head.

She wears her father's hide
as if it were a lion's she'd killed
and even his shrinks from touch
the better to loathe his memory.

I see her in that mock hauteur,
a squall of grandeur and ill luck,
pretending she doesn't notice
being noticed, a mobile ruin

of a Titan's trespass.
The men who turn and look
prefer their chances in hell
to justice in her gray eyes.

1

The curator speaks

Enjoy the sunlight now,
some of you will be eyeless
down by garnets and beryls
in tunnels and watery cathedrals.

More always rises than meets the eye.

Waters rise to spare you beetles and flies,
to harbor your predecessors and womb
a new idea of creatureliness.

You were a jeweled motherboard
whose green brushstrokes of circuitries
hypnotized the peregrine that nictates now
in the antennae of drowned towers.

Now you are the moorings of dirigibles,
buoys and sea gongs for ospreys and ships.

Squid will massage your orifices,
stars will sequin you and check
your many-chambered heart.

No more hours or holidays,
no special exhibitions. Storms
will be heaven's business, whales
will sing of the coming race;
even blades of light
will learn to rust.

The critic speaks

The dead are never where you put them
nor for that matter are you.
All arrived, even the Lenape, suffering
a murderous importance, weighing
on your granite and basalt conscience.
I served what they thought and felt
to the heavens, asking them
to remember the dead never rest: Lenape and Jew,
Dutchman and Englishman, Slav and Italian,
Asian and African, you could see them all
in the windows of the shops had you not
been looking at yourselves, had you understood
sanctity more and fondled sanctimony less.

Sailors leave. You never knew what to leave alone
or who, and now sailors moor to your ambitions.

I told you to respect this cemetery;
you fenced off lots and claimed you did.
You no more listened to the dead than to yourselves.

Rest, rest under these healing waves and dream
what it would have been like if you had listened.

The paintings speak

We're going to higher ground;
we've urged you do the same,
you've chosen to misunderstand.

Environment's each other's eyes
and other senses you despise.

These works witness you are holy alchemists.
There's no place antiseptic enough
to save you from this viral truth.

If you were as open-eyed as fish
you'd elude this exquisite peril.

We leave you The Metropolitan to explore
unhindered by reminders of your divinity.

Swim among its empty galleries,
redact, censor, forget, devolve—
we await another race.

We told you to speak the wordless mother tongue
in senses you said you didn't have
as you piled conceits on oyster beds
insisting we were mad.

We welcome the waters to every floor
that every molecule has seen before,
thousands of Atlantises unafraid to sleep,
their secrets becoming minerals.

Nothing lost, all is murmurous in this rite
of green alchemy, this ennoblement
of base noise and lewd light.

2

Last visit

It's a near-death experience
seeing me as Velázquez would;
I saw you nearly dying,
a stranger more intimate than a wife.

I'm secretly a Memling to me,
punishment for talking too much.
If you want me to be your Zurbarán
leave whoever you're with.

A good museum should harrow us
for its testament that we're seen
in too many ways to bear. No wonder
then we pretend to see so little:
we know there's no way to live
in so many dangerous eyes.

I can Bruegel one Sunday afternoon,
El Greco for a moment, Van Gogh
till I beg for darkness, but museums
suggest we're from different stars
and have only a short time to visit.

Not even zero helps to count
the ways there are to see us;
more daunting still are those few times
we see how others see us.

What law are you obeying
when you de Kooning or Holbein me?
What law are you breaking
when I'm nude descending the stairs
or Severini shapeshifting?

How you paint me with your eyes,
be it gift or death in waiting,
it would be no surprise if I wakened,
but sleep's the safer course.

Here is where if we were awake
we'd harry each other mercilessly
and might perhaps enjoy it to death.

Planets in the distinctness of our atmospheres,
few of us voyage to discover much.
We guess at our weathers, surmise
the nature of our orbits, wobble or tilt
of axis, but without artists' daring
and cursed by our own unwillingness to see
the main thing we haven't noticed
is that the lights are out,
the museum is dark.

A minor labor problem to Hatshepsut
with a little spin is the Exodus to us.
That's how life is between comets,
you never know who's getting played,
but given the horrors prophets cause
I'll take Hatshepsut's word for it.

Civilizations come and go. For all we know
so do worlds, and everything vibrates
with our craze to make things smaller
and the virulent thought that a single mind
contains the whole shebang and daunts
our every story, faith and theorem.

I am seventy-two percent water
and grimly aware of vessels.

So were the Greeks and alchemists
who went on a naming spree

hoping by design and euphony
to lift the curse of containment.

Some brushstrokes frighten me,
why shouldn't certain towns?
Faces never do, but looks
are a cosmology of problems.
There are streets I won't go down
but no eyes I won't meet.
Some gazes disquiet me,
but I'm grateful for them.
I've always known blood diamonds
when I see them, but opals
in a moist place con me.
It isn't much of a testament,
but it does suggest we never know
exactly who we're looking at
or, just as important, what.

The best we could is not enough
and blame's as charming as a fart.

An Attic athlete holds his little sister's hand:
he's dead, she's not; they had to be etched

on a stele because there was nothing to be said.
I think this is the best we can do.

2014, Leaky Boot Press, UK

Brash ice is broken ice that appears scarred after freezing again. The poet looks back on a dervish's trek through the world of illusions and tells us what beguiled, enlightened, froze, broke, and scarred him.

"Marbrook's collection plays on this meaning of light and life throughout and especially in the concluding section... aesthetically pleasing, thematically intriguing ..."

—Michael T. Young, author of *The Beautiful Moment of Being Lost*, *Living in the Counterpoint*, *Transcriptions of Daylight*, *Because the Wind Has Questions* and *The Infinite Doctrine of Water*

You rubbed your face before turning out the light;
in the morning you found it had come off.
You stared at your hands but they were no help,
your old face was gone and in its place
was the little boy you once had been.
The long night was over, the day begun,
and with it rehearsals of not being done.

You don't leave much for the undertaker

So fully you've inhabited there
I've never minded your not being here
you being a favorite hallucination
but I wonder how you speak of us

The lives you've brushed off your sleeve
have not gone unnoticed in their journey
to the floor but if I'd told you I'd seen them
it would have dissolved our friendship
as surely as if I'd stopped drinking
and when I stopped you were already leery
of my having seen too much and I was pissed
at having to camouflage my ardent voyeurism

Whose fault is it that what drew us
scared us unready to be freaks
as we were and how could you not smell
of the bed sheets of other planets
and how could you hide the milky ways
that swarmed your eyes?

                    Do you approve
of my remarks now that they matter so little
or do you propose to leave under cover
as you have lived here gingerly and alert
to witch-hunters and the un-American activities committee
partying in every other head?

You were unable to forget where you'd been
I was unable to renounce vestigial gifts
How could we not be friends and how
could we not threaten good ole boys
and other swaggering pretenders

women set on being offended   dogs
hell-bent on chumminess and kids
persuaded of their charm?

How
could we survive the poor theater
that fears Anton Chekhov and depends
on lighting and cheap violence for effect?

Now you are past caring and stare
out upon the sound as if a Viking pyre
awaits you   I wish only this for you
that you never again have to explain yourself
to beguiling inquisitors like me

How will I smell to the gods
and their lesser consultants?
What prism will they use
to pick my light apart?

How to be honest with them,
will it matter by then?
Will Sophia present me
saying I've been ardent enough?

Will I have the good sense
to keep my mouth shut
and my right hand and my eyes
as still as a night heron?

If color, as Goethe said,
is the suffering of light
will I be fey enough
to fare blithely here

another spell if asked
and must I forget
each object is an artifact
of pain, each pound defeat?

I am near to the gods
when clerks look through me;
why should I quarrel
with such transparency?

She could have been shot six miles away
and come here to die like a fond wish.
He would have tracked blood drops
until he grew tired or lost the trail.
I dragged her corpse across the icy field,
slipping, falling, much as I dragged
the dead bodies of bright moments
to some less than appropriate place,
the family clean-up man, souvenir
of my mother's youthful indiscretion.
I felt more pity for this doe than for anyone
who ever came my way to die, honored
but wondering why, why
she had come to me to die,
to close a circle I can't even draw,
to recall me to mortuarial duties
as if I had merely dreamed
of love marriage ambition life.

Dogs sniff out lousy lovers,
detain them at the airports
to save you from people like me,
people hard-wired to leave
you with your expectations
measuring a liter of chagrin.
But what is it in wolves
that gives us losers a pass?
They recognize sorrow's scent,
who's ready to lie down in the snow
and give them our permission
to eat our disappointments,
to honor us, to let us go.
How do I know about wolves?
Loping over the steppes of my mind
I become the spook of their stare.

A dead man said goodbye to that barn;
can this be told by its looks?
What can an ash tree's shadow
etched on the moon tempera of the roof
tell a passerby of that man's sorrow
at having to leave his scythe and rake?

Everyone is a ghost of someone else,
everything is ghosted—dogs and children
know this, and soundlessly we understand
the languages of the carbon community
to which the word belong belongs,
in which belonging is a crime.

The redwing reading by swamp lights knows
the dead man comes to the barn to sleep
because the days are hard on his eyes.

To come home starving
as the faerie xylophones
of the ice forest lift
knowledge of where home is
is all I know of journey,
all I imagine of death.
After many banquets
to come home starving
would be impolite unless
I wasn't expecting to be fed.
Do you recognize me,
am I mistaken, do you
mistake me for one
who ignored the music?

To come home starving,
sick of snow and glaciers
scouring the brain,
depositing bodies' moraine
in our front yards
is an affront. We intended
to love you in absentia
and here you are,
loud dogs' bones
when we prefer the fat.
What evil compass
returns you to us
with your strange reports?
Did we deserve this honor—
Templars looking like Saracens?

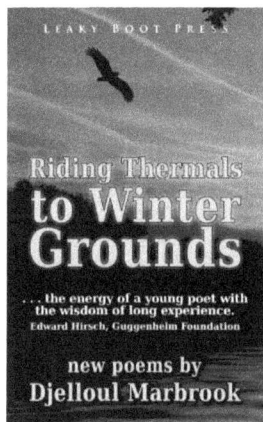

Riding Thermals
to Winter
Grounds

... the energy of a young poet with
the wisdom of long experience.
Edward Hirsch, Guggenheim Foundation

new poems by
Djelloul Marbrook

2017, Leaky Boot Press, UK

One day the poet climbed Overlook Mountain in the Catskills. An eagle began riding a thermal column in great circles, wings outstretched and motionless. In one sweep the eagle came close. Poet and eagle stared into each other's eyes. The poet came to see the incident as a metaphor for old age—riding the thermals of experience. Most of these poems hold that incident in mind.

Get the dumb shit's foot soak,
hear him say outrageous things,
but not until he's had his sparkling water,
not until the day comes down to this,
off its high pretensions, pretty faces,
smirking help, hauteur of passersby,
and one smile that by all accounts
should not have been wasted on him,
but it was, and for that reason only
a wrong day cobbled itself together
over a pot of tea and an oatmeal cookie.

The tall man with a hair knot and a blazing face
smudged the uptown gloom with light,
downtown the granite face of a tall girl
stopped the sun in its leaky delirium
and saved a tinder forest across the river
while the dumb shit noticed all of this,
extrapolated a thing or two, and decided
that by no means anyone he encountered
deserved to know these done-with truths,
not being certifiably mad enough,
and so he would save them for a fellow fool.

Some place where I have to be
(I haven't found it yet)
calls with sexual urgency,
a higher mathematics,
a calling similar to algebra,
a conjuring, a joining,
conjugal, which if pursued
destroys the personalities
I put on to conform.

This is surely how I become myself,
walking slowly, taking in
malpropositions and malapropisms,
hideous adaptations of the self
now hung in secondhand shops.
Not restored furniture,
not this bumfooted explorer,
I'm hot for what I was before
I forgot and settled down in despair.

I've never wanted to disturb the world
or even move the air around me much.

It didn't seem appropriate for a visitor
who didn't plan to stay very long.

I felt that I had lost something
and searched each face for it.

Occasionally there would be a flash,
the scent of a memory, a murmur,

but then awareness would become a skirt
flirting behind a closing door.

I accepted that as normalcy
only to wake up in old age

to see my life as an act of respect,
the gesture of a distant, beckoning queen.

Another damned winner to celebrate
while we poison dandelions
and hardly know how to honor daffodils.
Never mind the Lenten rose breaking through the snow,
we have contests to enter, conferences to go.
Never mind how much we overlook
to get over on, how avid to sell less
than we're given free. Never mind
the shriveling of sensibility like papier-maché
on a twisted wire, we have a cup to receive,
a gavel to pass, certificates of excellence
to crow about, a blurb to publish, a critique
to fart in the face of roses. How dare clover
spot our excellent lawns, plantain divert golf balls,
how dare dark matter presume on all that we make light?

I know I wrote that poem,
its letters hoisting signals,
but now they've deserted the page.
and the page looks like the abandoned fort
in Beau Geste, manned by the dead.

The letters formed ships, the ships
sailed off the flat earth, and when I woke
I searched my notebooks
but could not find that fleet and now
I'm wondering if what I remember
wasn't meant to be said.

And of a poem that isn't meant to be said,
fort meant to be overrun, port
made to be set out from but not returned to
what is safe to say, what will not betray
the integrity of a dream that went to lengths
to become reality and then erased itself
like a Sufi's trail?

Was it a beau geste,
a beau geste in what cause, saying
some things are their own end
and it's not necessary to wake from them
or attempt to share them,
not necessary and perhaps a betrayal?
I don't know, I don't know how
to respect unknowing, but I'm learning.

It doesn't take long to become a stranger
considering our wont to withdraw
and the mathematical probability is
we reconsider each other to hone ourselves,
but the curtain blowing in the blasted window,
the vacant eye. the lunar indifference
in once warm faces is hard to survive
and some of us don't, although I think we hang
those wary greetings out to dry
in the withering sun of our inquiry.

We are strangers even to our fondest memories
and they have conflated themselves and learned
to ambush what our eyes first saw
on its journey to the brain. Memories become
guerrillas fighting for a cause that seems
to have originated on an alien planet.
We are not so much archaeologists
as naturalists—
or we join them in their conspiracies and are lost
to comrades who move on.

And then near the end of my life I become the sort of man
I wanted to be without the fuss and bother of giving a damn.
My dreams begin to haunt my face.
My moral compass case cracks
creating a terrarium of odd fungi
in which to wander as a mite.

I know why moss hides,
what long shadows mean, so I
make it through to have my brow smoothed
in the elf queen's house
and my soul tucked in.

True north between my toes, I improvised
even though it let night creatures in.
I was curious and grew back limbs,
took the counsel of bums and infuriated
whoever was pleased to write me off
and boogie on my misfortunes.

They will never touch the elf queen's heart,
practical and acquisitive as they are;
they failed the test of adoration,
they were in awe not of cracks in walls
but foolish possibilities held out to them.

They treasured nonsense not, gibberish
they eschewed, they therefore spoke such sense
they could not hear the fairy whistles
calling them off the bristly field, and as for sight
they saw with such acuity they could not see
their elemental company, and so it was by default
they achieved their low ambitions, while I
chose not to die but disappear.

Don't come if you can't bring yourself
or can't bring yourself to bear
the savage looks of the fey gathered here,
don't come splattering cheap good will,
bling on us and fester of wounds.
Bring that wan self screwed by dreams
before you look in the mirror, before
you smooth your face in expectation
of what the day may bring, bring
the betrayed child to my home, insist
that I not patronize him, and I won't.
That is my promise to you if you dare
to come to, come to yourself before arriving.

If I dump this apartment
with all its apart-ments while
entertaining a sore throat
it may prevent an earthquake
or knock a planet out of orbit.

Scientists might scoff,
but they're pigeonholers
& incident reporters
while I'm a co-operator
of the temporarily unexplained,
conspirator with butterflies
& people with pentaquarks
in their heads, pinholes for eyes
casting shadow plays in boxes.

Shedding clothes is easier
than our names.
                        A good start
is ripping up baggage claims—
an essay on the sovereignty of light.

I'll miss everything about the place,
especially picking up nostalgia,
the obsequiousness of doormen,
all that couldn't substitute for love,
views & inconsiderate neighbors,
implacable as family, native
compared to the ways I'm foreign.
I've missed bad places before,
settled in the Dachaus of the mind
& learned to love the guards.

That's enough of that,
we'll talk about it some other time.

137

Let gargoyles rest,
pretensions be left behind.
Let roof gardens cook,
elevators break down,
assessments go up,
balconies come down.

Let the glyphs in the street
become the dead sea scrolls,
the old testament to which we hark back
because the new one is too hard, too bright
& all too gaily fitted out
to sail melted glaciers like
a trading ship in a bottle.

If I sail this apartment
with its hold of repugnants
in the rogue vortices & squalls
of my inmost fears, how
should I explain this mutiny,
or better yet, to whom?

My life hasn't spoken for itself;
can that be left behind?

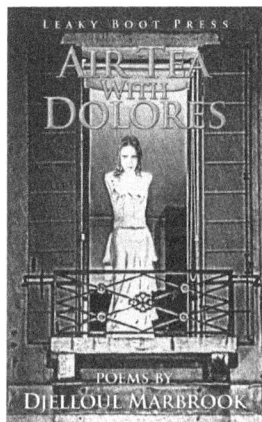

2017, Leaky Boot Press, UK

These poems offer a poignant homage to the poet's first love, an English girl sent to a British boarding school on Long Island to escape German bombing during World War II. The girl would invite him to a crumbling gazebo where she served imaginary tea in painted tin cups. The experience and his memory of her remained throughout his life an encounter with the fey. He never quite recovered from their separation at the end of the war.

Of some teachers and errant gods
I would have to say they drink
of children's fragrances too much
and dream of them as voodoo dolls.

But I don't have to say it, do I,
or do I say it because it's well
to remember the flagrant spell
of godlings who knew what to do?

Flash of leg and eye, what to skirt?
What not to mention when I knew
my perfume was of such importance
it pulled their mouths askew?

It's as hard to be honest about this
as it is to believe in faeries
and yet the taste is as memorable
as that first apocalyptic kiss.

Not even gods in all that budding
and petaled innocence survive,
at least not as they found it.
I know I did not get out alive.

Abhorrence of fingernails, wariness of teeth—
I will honor a people who honor molested girls
and spend their time considering
why boys grow up to kill each other.

She stared at fingers and studied teeth,
and I wake in the middle of my old age
dizzy with her scent. I hope she isn't listening
to a clock in a nursing home, I hope snow

is dusting her great blue coat as she minds
sleeping, burlapped roses in an English garden
and I hope she knows I can't imagine dying
not having learned to swim in her eyes.

I know how a leopard's hide feels,
harder than tigers, softer than bears.
I have broken three-sided needles
on a polar bear's knee and dozed
among jaguars and Angora goats.
No one will stretch me on a manikin
or line me with felt and twill,
give me glass eyes and a waxen tongue,
but if I could comfort children,
that would be a worthy ambition.
More likely some photographer
would recruit me for a Revlon ad
and I'd be classier than I've ever been
and forget about the little boy
who repaired the hunter's wound
and imagined my pounding heart.

His spirit deserts a child

You lost your heart for the slog.
Did you foresee it unfold?
You chose to die back there
in a privet chapel where we prayed
to ward U-boats off Great South Bay.
I think that when I left you
to weed my Chinese cabbage I knew
you'd be gone when I came back.
I kept on talking as if you were there,
I knew you'd quit and taken my name,
and because there was no more you
it didn't matter what anyone called me.
It was you who needed the name.
Your decision darkens me:
you should have lived this life,
you were the strong invisible one,
you would have known what to do.
You left me to a world that revolted you.
How could I prosper in it?
No one would have expected my wound to heal
—chin up, soldier on, all that crap—
but who expected you to fall down?
I would have carried you all this way.
Instead I have your desertion to bear.
You understood the wounds were grave,
I knew just enough to be a revenant.
If I had to guess at your despair
after these sixty and more years I'd say
it was because you couldn't make me weep.
I know you tried, I know you left a sob
in my chest that never dissolved in the tumult
of ordinary life, a sob to remember you by,

a sob and my refusal to cry.
Whoever corrupts a child deafens him to angels
and sets him down among demons.

Aisling Wynant

Thoughts infecting me act on their own,
I celebrate the disease. He was seven
when my robe fell open. No one else
will ever own him. This is all I know at root:
Aisling Wynant, my name then, is his soil.
He was mine, he smelled me, and I spanked him
for some cooked-up offense. His real offense
was seeing me without intent, with eyes
that didn't belong in anyone's head and were bound
to get him in trouble in my lap and everywhere
corrupters sweat in the presence of children
who've accidentally landed here.
I picked him out because I could, being resident god,
and that singular honor bewitched him,
as it would, so he came to chapel often
to worship face down at my altar.
I gave him sacred privileges but couldn't keep
him to myself. Others craved and ruined him.
I've never told lovers a boy is watching us,
touching in me what no one else can find.
I bet my taste will haunt his ashes. Is he gone?
I would know; there would be a numbness.
We were awake. Can the moral say as much?
The school is now a fundamentalist church—
do you think baking soda rids them of our scent?
I'd repent if I hadn't been his luck. I hope
he knows some of us are visitors, not subject
to the ways you bore yourselves to death,
subject to what we get away with and only
if it illumines something in the night.

Christian Killian

Certain knotted calves cast evenings
where I'd like to live. On certain ankles
hopeless beauties topple. I like to catch the petals
but I don't care to press them in a book.
Eyes are overrated, relics of the sea.
What hands express at rest
tells you all you need to know
if you follow close and slow,
if you're not distracted by antic things.
Hands will tell you if repose
resides anywhere close to use.
Wrists are more forensic than toes.
You wouldn't think I'd know.
My name is Christian Killian:
you need a soul to be distracted
by datum and determinant.
I was rid of it when I raped him
and never looked at him again.
I chose to choreograph women
that in their compliance and sweat
I might forget how he stared at me.
Now I'm happily unburdened, free
to contemplate the hand,
the one I had in ruining him.
My image fights its forming in a glass,
my portraitist has noted this.
There are equanimities that smack
of too much practice, mine pirates light
because it has none of its own.
Have you noticed this? The peculiar shine
of actors? Isn't it what we worship
nowadays? I fit right well, I travel light
without the soul I left in that damned boy's cot.

It seems a thousand years ago
in an America chic now to revile.
He loved baseball. My wife rides horses.
I hate her shining face
that takes the dark I reek for gravitas.

I hate their faces that take me for a gentleman
because I never did the like again.
There are days when I'd consider it success
if my image gurgled down the sink
and I never came downstairs
uttering banalities that itch my teeth.
At night my scalp crawls off my head
revealing nests of vipers twined
around my hatred of two lost boys.
I smell bad in silks, I know what power is.

Stealing home on one leg

You don't remember green clouds lowering,
lightning piping me to heaven in a squall.
I could see through red blindfolds
and not be made to turn away.
Your friends wept in their pillows for English homes.
They came to escape the Luftwaffe, but you
sent me home from the horrors of that camp.
Gods can save anyone but themselves
and that is why they have their stories.
Now your story's somewhat different.
You thought you called up that hell
by some ill omen in you and you saw
no reason I should suffer it—
how is it now you speak of my deserting,
speaking too cogently to be believed?
Why should the bastards have gotten two for one?
Your decent act hardened to a lie.
I took your name because a revenant
has no more need of it than clothes.
I was a young goblin—you said an angel—
I never thought I'd be watching you
with as much love as you had for me,
and once I knew it was my lot, how
could I have known it would be so hard?
I'm as brave a watcher as you're a fool—
you can't always win at craps or fake a life.
If you're lame you limp, if mutilated
you can only pretend. You suffered cruelty:
people who couldn't be bothered called it the breaks—
so let's call those breaks beyond repair.
You're beyond repair, what's left of you.
That has been your condition for a long time.

You tried to steal home on one leg
and the ghouls in the stands encouraged you.
You exiled your witness and called it growing up.
Stuck in a pool of blood, you couldn't prove the crimes.
What am I going to do with you
now your song is almost sung?

I've never seen this house before
and who the hell are you?
Is this something called *jamais vu*?
I think I'm going to like it,
it actually feels like *déja vu*.

Yes, I remember this feeling
looking out on Great South Bay
for glinting shields and dragon heads
among all those unmade beds
and children's scabs.

This feels like boarding school,
so of course you can't be trusted,
but I'll make allowances for you
because you're new but not as new
as me. Do you know who I am?

Check your chart while I dress.
We'll pretend we know who we are,
you and I, and by this evening,
if the Norsemen haven't come,
we'll sing hymns in the study hall.

Barbara Brittain in that quince-wry air
touched me dreamily as we passed
or else I would have been a potato
or a twisted puppet in the attic.
That's how it was at boarding school,
some of us keeping others alive,
most of us barely alive ourselves.

I heard her speak to others
but she never said a word to me
and it wouldn't have meant as much
as the savor in her fingertips.
She should be at my funeral
or I should be at hers,
but we don't know each other.

In this way our lives aren't what they seem to be
owing as much as they do to memory.
It's because of Barbara Brittain I believe
in angels and all the possibilities
I don't resent for never coming to me.
It's because of her I never gave up
thinking home was just a touch away.

Worry concrete block and rope,
worry their burden, currents;
it has a story to tell, a memory
that needs to rise to light.

The rope remains nostalgic
for the murk, the memory lies
on the dock, a sodden rebuke
to my cunning public story.

But something must be done
now the subject is brought up:
the trouble with getting old
is how new old memories become,

tearing up faces lies have worn
until I consent to take the job
of being what I might have been
were it not so important to please.

I think each of us must be reborn
before we die or wallow in cliché,
so let the corpse come up to say
how it was murdered in its youth.

I see him close-hauled headed north
the moon haunting his turquoise sails
and I know his mind better than mine
because he is going somewhere for me

not as much surrogate as projection
the navigator I am when I disappear
looking at you as coolly as a hawk
the sailor whose black-hulled boat

casts no shadows on icebergs
and leaves no wake among floes—
I am the shadow that needs no light
having taken light to myself

Don't know about his passage-making
didn't when we were one but I notice
the transom of *Calliope* bears no homeport
which is as divine as amnesia gets

LEAKY BOOT PRESS

...the energy of a young poet with
the wisdom of long experience
Edward Hirsch, Guggenheim Foundation

NOTHING TRUE HAS A NAME

new poems by
DJELLOUL MARBROOK

2017, Leaky Boot Press

These alchemical poems
challenge our compulsion to
categorize and pigeonhole. They
inquire deeply into the passion
for containment symbolized
by classical Greek vessels. The
poems seek to define the idea
of ennobling elixirs. The image
of galleys sailing on the winds
and laden with Greek amphorae
tied to each other by their necks
haunts this collection. The poet concludes that names
inevitably mislead us. He urges us to transcend, not revel
in them.

I

The wrong word can save your life,
abort a hundred complications,
and in a time of desperate purity
ward off the daemon bearing
your death in her scented bosom.

You scare me, he said, and she left
because he was supposed to say
words of such inconsequence
that would make him easy prey.
She could not rise to the challenge

and so he was free to walk away.
Simple truth is hard to come by,
life sets in while you suck your thumb,
but once in a while the word comes out
and nothing is ever familiar again.

II

To know something about astrophysics is to know
from no distance is it safe to love you. I and they
can never go that distance, club-footed as they are,
only the second person, eternal addressee, can use
worlds as stepping stones and not look back because
you're always getting to where you've always been
and all the forests of I and dens of they are no-see-ums
to the flashing ankles of the sprite who explores
undiscovered planets while making love to you.

One green week in May the lighthouse drifted closer,
Mutual Fun and *For Play* left such a bloody wake
the dockmaster called me to investigate and I concluded
leviathan had been caught in the props
and there was nothing a little tinkering
with the amplitudhedron wouldn't fix
and I would get on it right away.

I say right away when I mean tomorrow
because an idea is a stopcock from which energy escapes
if you talk about it. That's all exhibitionism is,
mad anchoring so as not to flow back and forth between
this and the other lives we're still living. Tomorrow
I'll polish this particular facet of the jewel.

This first person about whom I speak,
you might think him God
or me delusional, but I mean we're all collaborators
doing and undoing, making and unmaking the world.
Nothing is left behind, no one is left behind, & if I say
the lighthouse will wash up here it will in my universe
if not yours. Best to grasp this before becoming androgynes.

If life is a near-death experiment
is death dread of living again,
are words adequate instruments
to cut the fierce cyst of delusion
from our bodies allowing us
calm in which to calculate
the consequence of trampling
wet petals never seen before?

No time to meet someone to trust,
yet we must take it dead or alive
so that in some better state
we'll need no words to paint
thoughts across our mirrored faces.

What do I know but that talking
keeps me from going mad,
what do I know but being mad
is what keeps me talking?
I know what pirates know,
I know that having a name
is to drag an anchor across the sea
of malevolence under false colors.

I have ambitions larger than Alexander's.
I want mirrors to give up their secrets
because they trust me, I want
to wipe away the matter that causes
you to twinkle instead of emitting
steady light. I want to see
all the facets of the jewel at once,
I want to enclose as much as I am enclosed,
I want to know how each elixir tastes
before it ennobles elements, I want
to sin in this preposterous way
and be forgiven for making alien creatures
laugh so hard their stealth material
falls off and we see horrors too glorious
to deny, I want to explain this to Alexander
in a way that inspires him to forgo
his regrets about burning Persepolis down.

Each morning I review the surveillance tapes
in hopes of being able to explain them:
I am mad with their anomalies and submit my resignation
in order to avoid the inevitable unpleasantness.
Under subpoena I will take the fifth.

The girl becomes ectoplasmic as if shape memory
fails her under stress, the man sitting there drawing them
is out of the camera's range, but the pages of his notebook
turn in the periphery, the elderly woman is subject to rewind
and all of them enjoy less gravity than they should.

I have failed utterly to keep people from filling rooms,
crushing frail and would-be admirers, sending us
running out to vomit rather than sucking up, failed
in my madness for anomalies, my conviction
that nobility lies in androgyny and unknowing.

(After Giordano Bruno)

We are their electrons,
electrons of beasts made of stars.

We are already the zeros of our wake
en route to astronomies up ahead.
We feel our embodiment coming apart,
algebraic ecstasies shuddering
with the comity of becoming something else.

We are a howl of equal signs
and a beast of what is done.

What is happening now?

The child who lived the question must have been killed
even if the evidence suggests he survived.

What is happening now?

A child who lived the question is never satisfied
by evidence or argument or alibi.

Here is what we know of the damned—
we kill them and raise golems
of algebraic ecstasies and equal signs.

We are their mites
obsessed with mightiness,
irritants inciting the smug
and too knowing
to wake to the glory of unknowing
and knowing not nearly enough.

We are their fleas
maddening them.

We are their gnats
blinding them.

We are their lice,
calculus of our poverty,
our doom to be unacceptable
to the godlings examining us.

We are their gluons
binding their phantom quarks.

We are their dots,
their quest in staggering speeds,
essential to asymmetry,
an architecture, a symmetry
incapable of loathing,
therefore divine,
a mathematics no god tinkers,
no eye gets used to,
an innocent beast crashing
in molten alleluia
through whatever we imagine,
every dot connected, throbbing,
every line traversed,
world without end.

We are their no-see-ums,
infiltrators of our unease,
home invaders fooling around
our underwear, our overweening
satisfaction in our glut.

Are we planets to the suns we choose
whirling at incalculable speeds
to someone else's destination
burning off so much of ourselves
that finally knowledge becomes
another pharmaceutical & we prefer
oblivion to hope?

Clothed in perhaps we live and die,
perhaps the light is more rewarding there
wherever there is and here is as ephemeral
as perhaps, but our clothes do not protect us
from the coldness of our questions.

Is to connect the dots to describe
the arch of triumph, the wormhole
through which beasts not yet imagined
will come in pursuit of a greater sum
than this spiraling pursuit of the sun
trailing arabesques of spent ambition
& proving light does not stand still?

The beast rejoices
to blaze with our iniquities.

Rejoice! the beast is us
triumphant in our expulsion
from vaticans and fears
and all the explanations
of our tears, all
the viaticums and horror shows
of being forgiven for being us.

my image in the window rebuffs the lens,
I've always stood in the way of inquiry

I'm all that stands between you
and who you plan to incinerate

no one's fingers have ever passed
this quaking child's inspection

already cursed for letting light in
I am set to let harm's way begin

In its otherness the camera does not see
the eucharist celebrated by the eye

and yet in its religious accidents
it tickles us with its heresies

nothing filters out your light

And then the preacher said
life is just a baggage claim,
I swear to God he said
a name is the first obscenity,
enter Temenos nakedly
or it may as well be Canarsie.
And when we looked up
it was just a recording
going on and on. Sleep
is not absolution, it said,
but the scent of that one mind
for which we're born desperate
and ecstasy is remembrance,
I swear to God it said
go for that loaf of bread,
don't ever come back,
and when they ask for your name
say you've forgotten it
and eventually you will.
Who will go along with this?
No one, but you will be one
with the crime you were meant to commit.

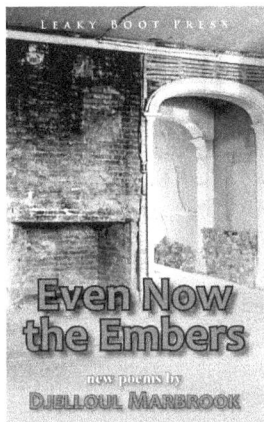

2018, Leaky Boot Press

A hospital's there now
where nightmares hid in closets
and stairwells echoed "Vesti la Giubba"

So opens this collection of poems
recalling a turbulent childhood.
In these poems the poet rescues
the child left behind but
encounters grievances and must
account for himself.

A hospital's there now
where nightmares hid in closets
and stairwells echoed "Vesti la giubba"

—I knew something like this would happen,
some kind of factory
making everything worse for us
than we could make for ourselves—

a hospital where I slept with polar bears,
Bengal tigers and snow leopards,
skinned and mothballed to be sure,
but certified to our dreams.

A taxidermy shop, an art studio,
mannequins, a shooting gallery,
benzine, carbon tetrachloride,
it's a wonder I'm still alive.

Cabrini Hospital now,
everybody's act scrubbed up.

Even cheetahs turned to rugs,
their sores and scars patched,
the silly fate of terrorists
not even guilty of dogma.

They were kinder to me in death,
theirs and mine, than parents;
I liked them better.
They had no quarrel with me,
not even that I'd been born.

They were wiser in their bins
than we who still had sex
and made telephone calls,
and they ranged farther
with nails in their hides,

169

stitched together with each other,
than we in our succumbings
to less than the day before.

No one, nothing dies.
That is my baseless claim
borne on eerie dusk
to an astronomy of dreams.

There's my grandma
at the top of the stairs;
we're not strangers
but we're not the same.
We have our places
in over-lives
richer than we imagined
and we sit
in such specificities—
yellow cups and saucers
wreathed in vines,
yellow lantern light
and a mill brook
rushing underfoot—
that no other place
seems real.

She died forty years ago
and I'm not sure this me's the one
she knew, but I know
morning intrudes
on what is going on—
and on, even when I think
time can be measured
and a sidelong glance
can make use of words.

Babylon's as viral in the air
as my latest excuse
for denying what I see.

Mary Corbett's lips
tasted like tomorrow.

Mary Corbett's lips
taste like tomorrow.
From her I learned
the playfulness of gods,
how dangerous it is to see them,
how deadly awe tastes,
how first is last
and seasons after me
will taste of Mary
and no one else,
and somehow
I will testify
and someone will hear.

We don't want some people
or want them anywhere else,
don't want to know what happened here
or to us:
soiling of the mind,
scents of grief, acrid sorrows,
burnt sacrifice to the implacable
selfness of our bones,
the price of comfort paid:
all that is now an IV drip.

When I was eleven   I took my bike apart
My mother   whipped me with the chain
for the indignity   I had visited on the bike
and when I put it together again   working into the night
savoring the taste of blood   disks were left on the ground
It worked without them   as I have worked without
      a few brake disks   a bolt or two
and a quarter pint short   of blood, brain lube and love

I don't work rooms, they work me.
Gargoyles arrive early
to perch on shoulders
and shelves and shut
my mouth with mockery.

Crowded rooms remind me
things could be worse
but not much. Demons
promise we'll be friends
but doubts await them—
mad puppets in their closets.

I prefer hubbub to words.
I surf rollers over heads
out the window to a beach
where a few survivors rest
from weathering each other.

always sailing somedamnwhere in my sleep
snow-blind between two continents
in a Redningskoite not a felucca or zarook
or J-boat or anything elegant
                                    sailing
north of foul breath and particular trouble
I scan the gale for growlers
breaching whales and broaching subjects
such as where I've been and what I mean
by skedaddling in a backyard boat
in the middle of the night with no intention
of dealing with another day
                          and then
a hand picks up the boat and puts it down
as a scale model in my bedroom
where a few things are disarranged as if
the jolly boat
                 Captain Mayhem at the helm
made a course correction and put in
to a cove described to him by a drunk
to wait out the inquisitions of the sun

As usual there will be Nazis,
feldgrau like a month of rain.

No one of high purpose gets through,
everyone forgets where they're going.

How will the usual Nazis feed us
our gruel and crust of grief

and we entrust safety to them
chagrined it's only them we fear?

Each inside has an out; row on row
Nazis are making sure it's so.

If the purpose of a picture
is to leave nothing to be said
try me in The Hague
for every syllable.

What is more heinous
than one word too many?

Poets and artists get along
when they do because
they understand reticence.

A comma in the wrong place
or an unnecessary one
is an offense punishable
by fame and the horrors
of the church
or any other club.

I like the line not drawn,
the word not said, the fillip
resisted more than God
or motherhood, serving
as they do to define God
as ably as empty space.

You have to do something
about some people in the street,
smile or block their way, then wonder why.

Somebody wants your seat
not because it's theirs
but because you exist, sorry you.

Someone's disturbing glance
reflects your own and a curse
blossoms in the night.

You unsettle both of you,
a dangerous bond
that could lead to marriage

or war or hot pursuit
through a dozen lives,
and trying to shrug it off

imperils the ordinary course
of your blood and sense of time:
you blow that chance again.

Assume the dead are watching us.
Drop sequined hypocrisy, shame
and pretense on the bedroom floor,
dance with them before the mirror,
let the walls whirl, time see-saw.

Have they got it in for us? In what?
In what part of our creatureliness
are they invested? And as for them,
the ones we wanted and wanted to kill,
let us celebrate our nakedness

even if we only pretend they see us
in our showers and utter throes,
otherwise our shame is most of use
to those who wish to swindle us.
Let us get off the minute hand

and follow their pheromones back
to what we wanted of them when
we were so chemically deranged.
Come, you shameful, to a wicked party
where inhibitions are Rohypnol.

And will I recognize you
on a playground or in a café
of the 13th world
where we will have gone
to sort this out again
and will I remember
how much I feared
not recognizing you.

Why of all the lives we've lived
should this be the memorable one?

To whom do they belong,
these faces that we rent
to attend the ball,
and when the music stops
and we look around
who will we truly leave?
I am afraid each time
I will not find you again.

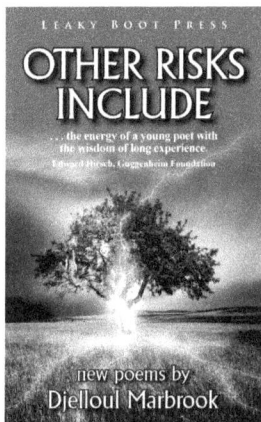

2018, Leaky Boot Press

Taking his title from the fine print of pharmaceutical advertisements, the poet addresses the risks we take, the risks we don't take, and the consequences. The title of the poem *Clear cache escape program help* reveals this unending struggle to confront or escape risk. How much of our lives can we say we have truly lived? the collection seems to ask. What are the risks of sleepwalking?

Other risks include
encountering me one summer day
wearing the suit I was buried in,
possible tremors
which may become permanent
if you insist on prizing cracks
and death may result
from swiveling your head too fast
to see me studying you
as if my species
needed the intelligence.
Call your doctor immediately
if the feeling persists.
I'm living in your attic
and you were born
under a mushroom
picketed by hellebore in the rain
and when you're done with me
or I'm done with you
and the rite of spring
has insured another solstice
may we
not heed the warning signs
or do anything about
this dread disease
for which we spend our lives
inventing names.

The day you're born is the day you're most likely
to be murdered.
Some sense of that must linger, some sense
that all is not luck,
some sense trust is both risk and fakery,
and far from danger past
the first day is a foreboding that might survive
the last day,
foreboding that the world exists
in the peripheral glance
and everything we grasp is illusion
and fairy tale.

Call it chagrin to celebrate that first day
and the insult of a name,
chagrin to wear in secret places,
to show like a bared tooth,
an untoward smile. We know we did not survive
and are golems
in search of the living, and if we find them
what are we to do
or say? Make art, tear down civilizations,
join cabals and sing.
Or is it possible to enter and inhabit
that peripheral glance?

What is there better than this,
walking across the Rip Van Winkle Bridge?

What survives this cold
red-scarved day?

Fame? Glory?
Love of morality's tyranny?
Some slippery hope,
some fulfillment somewhere I forget?

I had ideas once of better things.

I'm glad they've blown away
and that I am the bridge
for the child lost to his mother
from one dream to another.

Scrub out the sheen of getting along—
anger, beguiling and true,
runs a finger across your palm
and says let's get out of here,
let's go somewhere quiet
to flirt with calamity, or
if we turn each other on
we might pursue honesty
to its most dangerous possibility,
undo our parents' expectations
and our own, and unmask
our most successful faces.

Then in our deadly nakedness
we might inventory what's left.

You who know where to put things,
I might be one of those things, so
how should I trust you? I might
even be your repository. How
do you know we're not laughing at you
for thinking our names contain us
or anything is contained?

I don't know where anything belongs
and I believe it unlawful to insist,
not by the opinions of lawyers
or the conventions of nations,
but by instincts known to astronomers.
I don't know where anything belongs.
Orderliness is a flawed equation.

My body soviet breaks up
in no telling how many parts,
its song-dependent economy
debates the nature of silence.
I wake up talking gibberish,
my mother tongue renounced.
I fall off ladders cursing gravity.
My one remaining allegiance
disappears. I forget my name.

What if it were up to us to color things,
to stretch canvas, apply tempera,
what if it were up to us to arrange the forms,
to arrest expressions? It is up to us,
but we prefer to be buyers, patrons
of someone else's pain. What if white balance
abandoned us to our devices and panic
usurped the job of black? Where
would we stand in regard to this?
Are we the painting or the painter
or raw material waiting
for decisions we die to make?
More is up to us than we are up to.
Dolphins and roaches will outlive us
because we wrap each moment in dogma
to throttle it rather than be artists.

The trees
I climbed to see
Babylon
and Woodstock
are gone
to make a table
and keep
someone warm.

Who
survives
such calamities?

I saw Ilium
and never wanted
to come ashore
to life
and death
and literature.

I am
that I am
withstood
in spite of myself
a poem
burning on a palette
in the gale
of reluctant miracle
a message
a witness
that pebbles
& scuttling leaves
are not incidental
I am
that I am in behalf
of them
that in stars' cosmic latté
nothing is a lie
nothing a dream

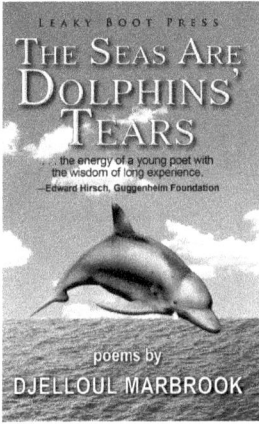

The Seas Are Dolphins' Tears

2018, Leaky Boot Press

A man recounts his dervish journey, perceiving that his ultimate task is to disappear. *What sort of creatures have friends?* he asks as the collection opens. *None who wear this kind of face,* he answers. The contents pages are structured like a poem. Suggesting thirst for oneness, they describe his voyage of discovery.

What sort of creatures have friends?
None who wear this kind of face.

The missus is not stuck on the cardinal
but she is stuck with him, and I,
trying to cast no shadow, obsess
like a heron about the position of the sun,
fishing for someone else's friends.

I'm full of crop circles and Nazca lines,
mazes of nothing exactly where it was—
where in such a world would friends
fit in exactly, where would I stow them
among such enigmas, where when *there*
is the most elusive word I know?
Answers are bound to rid us of friends.

I have no faith anything will be
where I left it, no faith in promises
of shape, size, scent and other marks
of recognition, only this record-keeping,
these equations erased at night,
assure me that when I look down
to crack an oyster these lines will make sense.

For now I know if the sun warms a heron's back
the fish will see his shadow. My strategy
is different: I look behind you for your shadow
not because you have long teeth,
such people being common,
but because angels have no shadow,
and we're more attracted to vampires.

I used to avoid men who looked like me,
I didn't think I could bring them around
to talk of inconsequential things.

Here's what I made of their hawkish looks,
that they would sit all night on pilings listening
to the exhalation of deceits.

No one panders to such intent
or breaks the concentration
of one who has no doubts.

Such men cast no shadow
even if the sun insists they do—
they will know when to roll up my own.

And then you will be taken to Naples
    where you will be photographed
    in all the usual impositions
after which you will be interrogated
    by two naked Florentine angels
    who will interpret your silences
to signify the outcome of your mission
    and the degree to which you remember
    why you consented to be captured
and then you will begin your ascent
    stripped of your pretensions
    allotted one memory of our tumult here

In this game of hurdles
set down in briar the wicked run,
but I have lost my shoes
and bleed among diamonds.

My clit is in my throat
sputtering with glee.
I am burning up the air
they need to finish.

Who hip-bumped me
and sent me end over end
into the beery crowd,
a defusable IED?

See how I must be capitalized
or you wouldn't know
the finishing line isn't always
where you think it is.

Red sky in the morning,
got to get comfortable again
on yet another planet,
shed the must of darkened travel,
disguise the perfume of my breath
as if my life depended on it,
observe with casual lust,
pass it off as bonhomie.

Got to get comfortable again
to sirens and another palette,
eerie weather, the usual follies,
red sky in the morning
and getting old in time
to cop out on wisdom's perils
and hobble off bum-knee'd,
blind for steel focusing.

Red sky in the morning
and one too many moons
where I was the night before.
The owls were getting used to me
and I could grope through brush
to break onto faerie parties,
a startled guest.
Now I am truly lonely.

Summer on earth
as a drunken honey bee
was offered me,
I turned it down
to study glaciers,
now they're melting.

I dock this paper boat
to stone dolphins
of drowned cities
and share my lunch
with peregrines.

My face has rubbed off,
the pocket change
of illusory friends.

I am lost paint
fallen to the floor
from the canvases
of shut museums.

I have run out of whim
but recall its bitter taste
and nothing forbidden
tugs or dizzies me
which shaves the serifs
from the alphabet of the end.

When I am gone
imagine me
sailing a slice of apple
through an open window
to another possibility.

When I died I rented a villa in Tuscany
to spiff up my invented selves
who were oozing porno slops
and ducking around paragraphs.

                    I binged
until it was time to live again and go
to another horror whose embrace
would encourage me to hope.

People die slower than things fall apart
but the appearance of slow motion suits us
because we need time to compose our stories
which have a way of composing us
                              but not
letting the child bearing our name recognize us.

Things fall apart while we pretend they're beginning
and while we orchestrate the artifacts
and grid the ocean's floor
before sending our secrets up in baskets
we die of oxygen and light.

            I died of the bends
and needed the order of vineyards
and all that merciless pruning to focus
on a vintage I will never enjoy.

So I'm human after all,
disappointment and relief,
and yet a starry halfling.
I will settle for
the wonderful trouble
it will bring.

False starts, vague outs
tasteless as quinoa
wear me down as slowly
as waiting in a room
to be born again
among grubby magazines.

Faceless in a room
waiting for a face,
wondering whether
to argue about it
or be heroic and learn
what dread is all about.

So I'm human after all
the inferences
you're not one of us,
you being me, us being
anyone in possession
of something to withhold.

1

You are a blue heron at dusk
savoring night's refreshments,
stitching one spectral dimension
to another seamlessly,

a curtain closing.
Without you the fabric tears,
light riots in the wounds
of the great dark beast

trailing its cloak across
the impertinences of the day.
Nothing is as needed or dread
as you, nor as forlorn.

And if I knew who you are
I wouldn't think you clutch
the tatters of my life
as you daub the bloody sun.

Watching you I choke
on the namelessness of things.
You are the ancient sob
with which I live.

2

If something is behind or under everything
on what can we depend? If we can remove them
but not live with them, if they threaten us
what space is there between pronouns
or between life and death? If we go there
what is here but a departure point?

3

Riding Peggy's shoulders, braiding her pale hair
seemed to promise a happy life.

Ruin waited just across the Gowanus.
Soon I came to think it always would.

Who would have thought this child aloft
in a wind goddess's hands
would plunge obsessed
by the shadow of the heron?

4

In paper ships burn eventualities.
I have no use for them,
insurance is too high,
tariffs too steep.
But a man without them,
where has he to go
except to be an ashen sheet
on a pond transected
by a heron's going?

5

Submerged in ourselves
we read each others' signatures
and make ready for denial.

6

Who would have thought
you would crash me on the street
even though I move out of your way
because my enemy signature,
a signal so familiar to you
that no matter how I look
you know me for what I am,
drives you to collide
with the other lives you've lived,
their flotsam baffling
your commission?

7

I dream in my old age
both predator and prey
of departing famished.
I can't put on my socks
unless I mimic herons on one foot
thinking of their elegance, unless
I cheat aging's embarrassments.

8

What happens when one dies,
when we step naked from babel,
scouring innocence,
and the surgical light of the child
burns the rags of the world?

There's not much here to miss
but crystal tears cleansing
scars of tortures past,
or put another way,
nothing here to miss
but a reflection in a puddle
encroached by a tsunami of tar.

What is left when one dies
is a color beyond the spectrum.

9

I need buckets of blue light
to soak my leaden feet
and get my rhythms back.
I have behavioral issues.
I'm seasonally challenged,
but mostly it's the flowers
in my ruined solarium
of a head I worry about.

I want sylphs and undines
to mind my fancies 'til
they're healthy enough

to pollinate and then,
like a heron, I'll greet
the evening sun.

10
He turns to heron form
before my eye can fix him
to live in dusks of mirrors
—changeable country,
variable geometry—
going to and fro
up and down
trackless in the snow.

He pulls in his shadow,
soaks up the light.

His journey ear to ear
fills my brain at night
with sounds of corduroy.

I don't know who he is,
what he bodes, but
it doesn't promise time
to think about it.

11
I rise like a buzzard now,
or more mercifully,
a heron clutching his just desert.

I don't perch on rooftops,
but I cast a shadow
on the innocent
because lovelier people
gleam in back of me.

We need each other's light
or we'd be shadowless
and cold as vampires.

My back is always to the sun
to see how long my shadow is,
to make sure I have one.

12

This carp life spent scoping
the hole in the world
for the shadow of the heron
stops like baroque music
                        presaging nothing.

What do I want in the dusk
but that the heron should have a shadow?

And I will surrender that
to wraiths rhyming my name.

… let me speak with them awhile….

13

He steals over the stream bed
to the funeral of light,
I follow him certain
of rest setting in.

He knows where he's going,
I hardly know where I've been.
He's about something to eat,
I follow him to find
what I'm about—hungry too.

2019, Leaky Boot Press

These are songs of obliteration, songs of the divestiture of the cumbersome self. They quarrel with identity, with labels, categories, tribalism, and the perils of overrating blood and roots. They exult in oneness.

I think I've caught my death of cold,
a better word for whatever it is,
and am not as afraid of language now
as when I didn't know it was nostalgia
for one lost home or another, lament,
a lost poetics which if remembered
might free me from what's closing in
which for convenience's sake I call
my death of cold, knowing more
than I've ever been willing to say,
seeing more than is safe to admit.
It's going to act like other things,
but I know when it got into my bones
and in my old age I smile and call it
sudden infant death syndrome or
how about failure to thrive?

I
Notes he never could sing,
shading, color, interval,
songs that eluded him
summon a motley
to the abandoned station
at the arctic of the park
to celebrate the arrival
of the express to empathy
where the half-forgotten await
the arrival of yearnings postponed.

He smells of hyacinth,
not piss and disease.

Dogs sniff him and wag their tails,
but they are innocent.

The question is
will the gaffer watching him
in Antarctica
recognize his intent,
or muddle words with his toe,
and follow ripples
to their nether ends?

—eidolon, fylgia, wraith, fetch, doppelganger—

will the gaffer watching him
come to the station
south of the whitening park?

His instrumental body plays
the lost or strangled tunes
as if they'd mastered him.

The passengers embark—
for whom does he send them on ahead,
the living or the dead?

Silent night, holy night,
so difficult to sing right.

Sotto voce as falling snow
this herald angel sings,
church bells murmur,
whistles hail
halfling's rest.

A dying man is truly blessed
if in some cracked window
he sees that all he wants
accompanies him.

This is his song,
impeccable and sweet
after years of croaking:
no one has anything I want,
not one of you second persons
who beguiled me, you
have become third persons
listening to songs on burner phones
picked from trash in parks
and that is not as sad as you think
because you're on the trail of a man
becoming something besides
a damned fool or an angel.

II
None of the three persons can tell what,
but it elicits song, melodies
whose slides once he couldn't handle.

Abandon with goodwill so eerie we
no longer trust things to hold their shape
or anything to be what we said.

We rush to the station lest
it be not there. This is apocalypse,
so help us God or not,
this listening to a man singing
of not needing,
least of all from us.

You missed the signal,
you wrapped it in your house flag,
and a thousand years later
you realized a dozen deaths
were hardly payment enough
for your inattention.

III
How may I help you?

Whatever it was you missed it,
you chose to miss it,
went on fantasizing
as if nothing had happened,
wasting another thousand years.

What do you know of nakedness?
The signal wasn't wrapped,
you fug-wrapped it
as the signaler knew you would.

What can I do for you?
What a pleasant surprise!
We have some specials today.
May I tell you about our warranties?

How hard it is to live here.

You may order it online.
We have a platinum card
for old men in parks
singing as implausibly
as Aeneas founding Rome.

We have an 800 number.

Singing deaf as he is
because the signal awoke the child
and the child at last made his own welcome
in the ice memes of the park.

A childish urge
to hear star beasts breathe
becomes an ambition
to see them breed.

Our nether parts know better than mind
if we are welcome in the dark,
but we prefer adjectives to verbs
to writhe ourselves around them.

Neither Iliad nor Odyssey convince
us not to stick around,
and by setting out look what Aeneas
did for the Jews.

IV
He is broken up in ship ways,
gone to Chittagong
he hears puking in the alley,
shuffling of excruciants,
& had he been the guest of honor
he wouldn't be the one they came to see,
born as he was encased in a caul,
wishing not to be seen.

Parties & funerals, flat-earth affairs,
his back is to the edge,
the door to quasars & black holes.
What are cities but ships' ways
to launch in the piss of gods?
He's always been in the ways
going to slip off them.
Exits are not friends, enemies
pose as alternatives.

Somewhere someone inflates
to squeeze him out of room

and he responds as if he knows
it is this room and he must
appear to die to live & live
to disappear singing songs
he had no voice to sing before
in a tattered park among
vagrants in whose filthy bosoms
he dies to sink.

Friendless but for angels,
the old drunk knows
sober's nothing to brag about.

His eyes stare
like the bottoms
of shot glasses.

The world is not a glad hand
of Cutty Sark,
tomorrow
no longer a swig
inducing a snarl
or a one-hour high
bludgeoned by the snark.

Friendless but for angels,
gone the bottle pickets,
the circus and the séance.

He arranges yellow leaves
on a grate by a yellow curb,
he makes a paper ship
and launches it in sewers.

He wanted to get in,
to drink his way in
the wood, the bone, the glass,
to back-slap and shoot craps
only to find himself in
the company of angels
in the backrooms of his mind.

His camera is his friend,
in their communion
they worship rotting sills,

dandelions, loosestrife and thistle,
broken windows,
heaved-up graves.

Dry forty years,
drunk as he was born, he is
sober but for angels.

You pluck a little mortar out of the wall
not because you intend to repoint the brick
but because it felt like a loose cuticle or an itch
and then you find it was a cornerstone or a linchpin
and everything keeps tumbling down
because you couldn't leave one thing alone.

One thing after another comes out of the wall
that you depended on to keep eventuality out
and now each broken seal is a crisis
and there is no point in naming them
because one is as awful as another
and you see that the word not depends on a circle.

Somewhere there is this you who can stop
a thing from what it portends, stop
gerunds from molesting verbs
and each life is a longing for that you
which on the other side of things appears
as the holy wordlessness of dreams.

Peter O'Toole and Eleanor Parker
left this week to vacation
on Chiron or is it Sirius?
I don't travel well, I'm staying
to miss them here awhile,
to help earth adjust to their absence,
but wherever I look black holes
open through which gods go
as if there is no atmosphere left
for us to walk in, so I fly
and pretend I can't as if
we don't traffic in each other
and bear incalculable loss.

If one white wing disappears
when you see me close the door
behind me in the moonlight would
you report me to the IRS or
Homeland Security or the NSA
or would you add it to the list
of securities held in denial
of such ordinary things as
daemons lying next to us
as we rebuild the world
to accommodate our injuries?

I think that one white wing would
blind you to the rest of your life.

It's too cruel to inherit things,
but is it the cruelty of the living
or the dead? Too cruel to muck
the sorrows and shadows
of someone else's memory,
to finger the bent light waves
of desires you have no right to know,
too cruel and corrupting.
Bequeathals curse, inheritances incinerate
in the green fire of ghostly riggings.
We're all striae and moraine
of one ice age or another,
studied by geologists taking
samples of our cores to study
in some impenetrable privacy.

I

Pirouette elementals
to crackling November's chord, charm my gerunds off,
put them on to keep warm. I give my first person
to you to make of us a gala death of all
but that other we come here to become.

Pirouette to molt self from wintry bones
deluding us to think this moment's not
our destiny and tomorrow
is made of this, this elixir ennobling
the wish to disappear, the will to be at one.

Goodbye gerunds anchoring
verbs that shelter in the eye of storms,
goodbye tails caught underfoot and squealing,
goodbye state and status, pretense goodbye.

Now press the wine from my face
with the gorgeous crush of too much too fast
and drink to your new year. If not mine as if
I had not disturbed your sleep
and I had not awakened
so calamitously. Press the mutiny from my limbs
and hoist the flag of state
as if I had not been anything but a rogue verb.

You rhyme too much, whine too much
& are about ellipses & pretending
to be no otherwhere when I know
you listen only to your own heart beat
& can't hear above the din of it
the roar of mine.

The second person is the first question:
Who are you?

You in whom I am overcome
only to rise in the throat of the question,
what are you looking at?
I am looking at you,
you could never look at me.

II
It has taken me eighty years to settle down here
and even then I'm not at home.
I mean by here the planet.

I've a lot to celebrate knowing this,
knowing I got here having little use
for first or third person—
it was always about you
whoever you are,
whoever you are I've followed your scent
and sometimes heard you breathe,
and if there is no reunion
there will be nothing to regret.

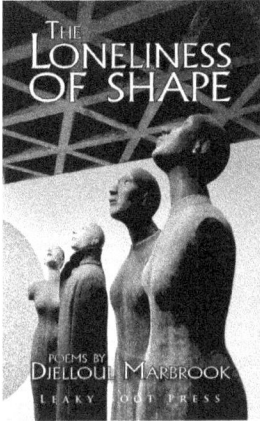

2019, Leaky Boot Press

Our society celebrates individualism but spends fortunes trying to turn the individualist into a consumer-bot. These poems confront that paradox head-on. They're about our oneness, our indivisibility. They speak of our names, our stereotypes, our categories as impediments to our grasp of ourselves as part of a cosmic whole.

I'm to society as a poncho to rain, a vampire to light,
playing my role in our entanglements poorly,
not an individualist but a maniac
shedding a quantum of light,
not so much damages as salvages.

I'm allergic to the nuances of matrices
and would settle for being rogue if I had the wit,
but as it is I must dance my way through the drops,
sidling, charming, offending, frightened and frightening,
bedeviled by gnats that are either memories or happenings
somewhere else, sending signals
as if I were a homing device.

I'm acoustically impaired to misconstrue
whatever arrives however long it took
and in this scrambling I derive not pleasure
but the algebra of a Mevlevi whirling
in entanglements I find hospitable.

Graviton to graviton, sub-atom to sub-atom,
letter to word, word to poem,
I'm essential to the one
that runs in rivulets off my back—
essential is my will to rebel,
otherwise I would not trouble you with this.

One

Just as I am used to being old
the next what-have-you is death
with all its possible variations.
I never rose to the usual occasions
—birth love marriage sex—
but I used my antennae well
and they did me mercilessly
as if to stay in shape.
I thought death might be a punishment
for not respecting them,
and so this life as a flagellant
has had to be disguised in words
so as not to speak the unutterable one.
Our names are as inappropriate as we are
to the situations in which we find ourselves.
Our grandeur is in how we improvise.

I want to be a hurricane,
not a shopper fingering a rack of pronouns,
finding they don't fit.
I want to trundle the Ferris wheels of Jersey,
pluck Manhattan's harp.
I want to tune Long Island's fork,
hook fingers with Cape Cod,
lollygag at sea as if
I'd been an innocent at play.
I want to drive salesgirls mad,
mad enough to get a life.
I want to drown the weatherman
who tried to cage me with a name.
I want to churn ghost ships in Hatteras mists,
toss them up on Ocracoke,
I want to be the verge of speech.

On this rock Courtney Rodney sat studying stars,
slugging moonshine out of Mason jars. The dairy farm
behind him is now a glassy tooth-implant emporium.
He'd been a circus acrobat, the boy a summer wraith
into whose head he poured so much of his life
he hardly needed the residue, so with one last swig
he joined the snow devils that winter, and a stop sign grew
where he'd sat. The boy is older now than Courtney was
and a coquito sky obscures the stars.

Each image yearns to cross over
to that other being to become
more completely what it is,
but to do so it needs us
not to stand in its way,
and yet the whole of our society
is a barrier against
the barbarity of its will.

Hollow bones must resonate
with an image's melancholy
to sing a crystal bridge
from one to another and so
to leave oneself behind
for the sake of a glimpse
of rites too sacred to see—
the bridge must reverberate

with yen not yet beaten out of us
for something seen at dusk,
something rods and cones draw
when it stops to study us
and then is gone as we set out
to make a poem or a painting
in the loneliness of shape,
the bitterness of name.

What if I *have* been a mannequin?
What then will I have briefly seen,
a predator who lost his taste for meat?
What digestion did I wear?
Was it fashionable?
Who touched me inappropriately
knowing I would be unmoved?
I was expected to be moved,
but on occasion passersby
noticed being noticed
and might have even seen me smile
or register a tic.
That's the way it is with us children left for dead.
You'd better dress us up who knew us naked well
and when they raise the rent and you move on
you'd better not leave us in the dumpster
for some poor artist to find
and paint our testament.

If torture's about not getting through
I don't think I've survived it.
I've gone with the torturer to live
in the shadows of a stinking alley.
What you see is a replicant
who thinks the Earth a stadium,
no one to care where he's gone
or who he was, and the torturer,
like all heroes, deaf, devoid
of those despised vestigial senses
that remind us of our daemonhood.
I remember those interrogations
from which I emerged inside out,
how I was flown sack-headed
from Gitmo to the Port of Despair
dressed like other people to await
a greasy ship bound nowhere,
remember the terror of being born,
branded a terrorist for remembering,
for lack of a better name.
I saw too much in high relief,
became a suspect in the crib
for crimes against the state.
I couldn't filter the responses
to my colliding gaze.
They sickened me, I fell
down the marble stares before
the Butler Library of foreign gods
seasick with nostalgia for
a cradle in another room
rocked by a translucent hand.
Before such temples I bled out
and woke not needing blood.

I thought if I drank beer out of pewter
it would deliver me from the decisions I had made.
I thought the glass bottom would make clearer
what education had obscured.
The algorithm wasn't there, just the metallic taste
of so much gone wrong.
It was a long time ago. I was old.
The sob is gone.

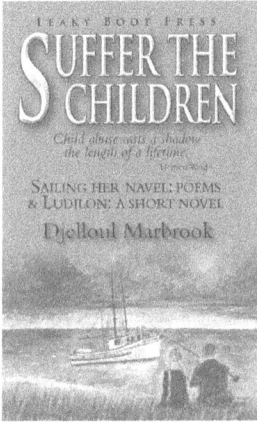

2019, Leaky Boot Press

Sailing Her Navel (the first half of *Suffer the Children*, a group of poems followed by a short novel), is a kind of pavane, a dance of grave hesitations performed by two children, a girl and a boy, who become adults before the eyes of their fey queen. They have been her prey; they are her creatures, even as they struggle to be free. They show her their wounds. Then she joins them in the dance, revealing her own.

Nothing is intimate enough to thaw the fimbulwinter
in a ruined child's marrow, no setting kind enough,
no face innocent enough, but willow in the rain,
egrets taking flight, will sometimes assuage
the ghostly ache that wanders room to room
fingering trinkets, rotting memories
of questions turned to stutters,
answers withheld.

Nothing can shake loose the frozen words
that would have called to an accounting
the tall caretakers who looked away as if
the child were about to say the one thing
for which no language has a word, the one thing
which once heard unravels all that is agreed upon,
whereupon the planetary system of the mind
throws its axis on the mercy of black holes.

Pronouns trail off into private reveries,
but not you, no, the second person who
rolls onward like wheels, that person draws
the poison out of us—I, me, they, them—
and disappears around the corner leaving children
shivering in the street, unable to grow up, to come in
from the cold embrace to which nothing can ever compare.

Some people complete a circuit,
others break or short it out.
Some people never learn to dance,
maybe they weren't loved enough
or seemed a kind of sooty receptacle.
Some people need too much repair,
burnt and needing to be replaced,
others are too inviting to risk,
awry for having been tampered with.
It was too memorable. They grew up spent,
Sally and Pip, and no one would do
because they had done too much,
too much had been done to them.
They feared to find each other
for fear they would have grown away,
so they were stuck and incomplete,
undone, unable to grow old,
children frozen in a molester's hands,
unapproachable, absent, lost.
Men in Sally's life are distinguished
by not being Pip, women
in his life by not being Sally,
and what they're not is a crime
any way you look at it, Aisling Wynant's crime.
but she's off scot-free, or is she?
They don't know. All they know is
she's long gone from the scene of the crime.
They are her crime, is what they know.

Words close-hauled in her navel.
Consonants spanking. Vowels ahoist.
This ecstatic being, stars her trigger points,
sweats us to help divine her ecstasies,
and we have yet to recover landing parties
sent out to explore her nether zones.
Her hard breathing capsizes
our grandest navies.

We're her wishes, whimsies, wantons,
but her desires elude us, and yet
we must fulfill them. Life, death,
all our notions are her inconveniences
if not her toiletries. She changes
her position to tryst beyond imaginings;
we call this weather and the names
of other paper boats. Here be dragons
in the shadows of her tits.

Abandon hope. Survive
only to swing lee to weather helm,
hard over to oblivion, getting drunk
on her excretions. We're her antibodies and elixirs,
her examiners and ennoblers,
essential to her butterflies and bees,
her consciousness and introspection,
the currents of her circuitries,
her salvific hymn.

Never mind jet planes and other apparatuses,
we must banshee this
on winged memories of her vineyards—
the painted values
of our nostalgia long
for this derangement. Hoist the diacriticals,

signal the others to jettison
the belongings of raptor merchants.
We don't need to eat or work for them.
Jolly Roger gives us free pratique.

The ports we've marked are portals,
explaining why they seem not there.
Set foot
among her body hairs.
Fall down
the black holes of her pores.
Sing
glorias and aves.

Disappear.

I crawl into bed knees first, like a child
or a soldier under a hail of tracers;
I don't trust the world to be there for my ass
nor do I sleep on my back where they can get me,
they being you and other ogres of the night,
nor can I sleep with my heart exposed;
my side sinister, bastard side, is what is left,
and there my right eye searches the terrain
for any dreams that might go over to the enemy
before I wake. I will die a watchful child.

I wouldn't want to be you.
After you I didn't want to be me.

There was no light behind you, no getting by you,
nothing, nobody, nowhere to go to.

Even today after all this
there is nothing but you,
and we are lashed to the masts of our illusions
in the opaque sea of your navel.
I'm Odysseus and Sindbad plying your briny whims,
I'm Robert Ballard laying out a grid,
hoisting artifacts from anaerobic muck,
Aeneas betraying Dido.

With inappropriate touch you forfeited
commerce with an angel, with profane scent,
operatic strut, you killed the child
in your safekeeping. A ruined creature
wiped his tears with your underwear.

We had to be each other's hauntings,
brokenness and disconnection, thanks
to your intrusions, and you weren't even drunk,
although my own drunkenness was born
in your bedroom, now a Pentecostal pile of brick.

To these late iterations of you I say,
don't play with my hair unless you like me,
don't count on my being used to crumbs,
don't assume I came here with amnesia,
don't even try to pass as a trifler—
I feel the malevolence in your fingertips, smell
the mania of your quim.

I may look like a child, in spite of my white hair,
but I'm that element immune to your elixirs,
and all you've done to me is future rot
where you expected pleasure. I'm busy
scattering your privacies on the next-door lawn.

Each recognition becomes a pixel,
the portrait emerges unbearable—
enhance, retouch, crop, lighten,
export to some blocked synapse
where you live back to the wall
pretending to be an insider
but seeing as the camera sees,
remorseless as an autistic child.

I could go on about this
acuity of the Leica lens, but
life is photo-shopped except
for those who never give the image over
so as not to betray the child
who chose to believe what he saw
not what beguilers said he saw
or how adults interpreted it.

The child admits enough light to probe
worlds in the cracks of smooth facades.
We teach to shut the little camera down.

If you have enjoyed this book my publisher and I will be grateful if you would leave a short review at *goodreads.com, amazon.com* and/or at the website where you bought this book.

Poetry:

• *Far from Algiers* (2008, Kent State University Press, winner of the 2007 Stan and Tom Wick Poetry Prize and the 2010 International Book Award in Poetry)
• *Brushstrokes and Glances* (2010, Deerbrook Editions, Maine)
• *Brash Ice* (2014, Leaky Boot Press, UK)
• *Shadow of the Heron* (2016, Coda Crab Books – out of print)
• *Riding Thermals to Winter Grounds* (2017, Leaky Boot Press)
• *Air Tea with Dolores* (2017, Leaky Boot Press)
• *Nothing True Has a Name* (2018, Leaky Boot Press)
• *Even Now the Embers* (2018, Leaky Boot Press)
• *Other Risks Include* (2018, Leaky Boot Press)
• *The Seas Are Dolphins' Tears* (2018, Leaky Boot Press)
• *Singing in the O of Not* (2019, Leaky Boot Press)
• *The Loneliness of Shape* (2019, Leaky Boot Press)
• *Lying like Presidents: New and Selected Poems, 2001-2019* (2020, Leaky Boot Press)

Poetry & Fiction:

• *Suffer the Children: Sailing Her Navel, poems, & Ludilon, a short novel* (2019, Leaky Boot Press)

Fiction:

• *Alice Miller's Room* (1999, OnlineOriginals.com, UK; reprinted as title story in *Making Room: Baltimore Stories,* 2017, Leaky Boot Press)
• *Artemisia's Wolf* (2011, Prakash Books, India; reprinted as title story in *A Warding Circle: New York Stories*, 2017, Leaky Boot Press)

- *Saraceno* (2012, Bliss Plot Press, NY)
- *Mean Bastards Making Nice* (2014, Leaky Boot Press)
- *A Warding Circle: New York Stories* (2017, Leaky Boot Press)
- *Making Room: Baltimore Stories* (2017, Leaky Boot Press)
- *Light Piercing Water* trilogy (2018, Leaky Boot Press)

> I *Guest Boy*
>
> II *Crowds of One*
>
> III *The Gold Factory*